My Journey Home

Memoirs of a Shetland Exile

My Journey Home

Memoirs of a Shetland Exile

James A. Pottinger

The Shetland Times Ltd.,
Lerwick.
2021

My Journey Home
Memoirs of a Shetland Exile

First published by The Shetland Times Ltd, 2021

ISBN 978-1-910997-33-8

Printed and published by
The Shetland Times Ltd.,
Gremista, Lerwick,
Shetland, Scotland ZE1 0PX.

CONTENTS

INTRODUCTION

Often, when describing to friends lifetime events sufficiently striking as to bring sharp recall, I have been told "you could write a book!" At the age of nearly 86 years and inevitable mortality drawing ever nearer I decided that it was now or never.

Perhaps the main difficulty is that many of the sharpest memories are of events related to my varied work experiences at home and abroad, and whilst possibly of interest to some a general reader may find these tedious. But I hope not.

I guess over my lifetime in comparison to some I have been lucky. Born into a caring family with strong sense of what was right, I enjoyed a happy and long-lasting marriage, and was similarly fortunate with a supportive and attentive son and daughter-in-law and blessed with a special granddaughter. Added to this were a number of satisfying and rewarding jobs since the age of 16 years and, to date, I am doubly fortunate not to have had any serious illnesses apart from the usual aches and pains that come with age, plus over twenty years of retirement to enjoy my good fortune.

Starting in my teenage years when going to the gym three times each week with some pals when serving my marine engineering apprenticeship in Greenock I have fortunately been able to maintain this exercise routine, although with some gaps owing to change of habitat. One factor which might have helped may be that I have never even tried to smoke, and I am still able to continue this activity albeit inevitably at a much lower intensity, although I am usually always the oldest participant now wherever the location. So hopefully all the pain has resulted in some gain!

When in the merchant navy, on one ship, along with the fifth engineer officer, we managed to cobble together some barbells from various lengths of round bar and blank flanges to allow us to exercise, the chief engineer opined that obviously we were not being hard worked enough in our daily duties.

Luckily I have always had active hobbies such as gardening, caravanning, photography and boating, and have had published seven illustrated books, four depicting Scottish fishing boats, two of Clyde shipping and one of Shetland views and text. Having always been interested in draughtsmanship and free-drawing and painting I have contributed probably something like 600 ship and boat model plans for three UK model magazines since the middle 1970s and numerous articles for shipping magazines. I continued my schooldays' hobby of drawing and painting ships and boats and have completed many paintings for skippers and owners, mainly fishing boats.

Initially I only used water colours but after my wife bought a set of oil paintings whilst we lived in Holland I took up this medium. Watercolours are unforgiving in that it is difficult to correct without spoiling whereas with oils you can just paint over any errors or start afresh.

EARLY DAYS

First things first. I was born on the ninth of November, 1935, in a small flat-roofed extension on the back of Johnny Ward's house at Highmount in Hamnavoe, and lived there until I was about three or four years old. I went back to have a look a short time ago and noted that this has been replaced by a larger extension. We then moved to the most westerly house at Branchiclate, where we had the south end with a small adjoining closet and front porch. Alex Jamieson, Joanne Maggie and family lived in the other end which also had an extension at the back, this being basically a crofter's but and ben house, now a gradually reducing ruin, which incidentally would be an ideal site for a new house.

I wonder if this photo of me was taken by Clement Williamson, it looks like a posed photo.

**With my mother. I fell off a seat in Gilbertson Park and
broke a collar bone, probably around 2½ -3 years old.**

I would have been two-and-a-half or three when I fell off a
seat in Gilbertston Park in Lerwick and broke my collar bone.
For some reason I can still vividly remember my mother
carrying me into Dr Lamont's surgery which had patterned
glass panes in the door.

The owner of the house and adjoining croft at Branchiclate, Tony Henry, who was then living in a house behind Halcrow's shop and former kiln at the lower end of the Glen, decided to move to Claet so we had to move out. We then moved down to the beach where an extension was built on to the south end wooden house belonging to my Pottinger grandparents just above the beach, and a door was knocked through for us to get access to their ben end. This would have been about 1941, the house remained in this state until much later a large extension was built on the back with two bedrooms, kitchen and bathroom.

The house at Branchiclate where we lived circa. 1938-1941.

Grandparents Jerry and Margaret Pottinger.

Being born into a fishing family and brought up in a small fishing village in one of the UK's most northern archipelagos, one's early training and instincts were fishing for such as crabs and coal fish, and handling of small boats under oar, sail and motor all coming second nature. Even our childhood pastimes were inevitably centred on play involving depictions of boats and ships of varying types, including "skeety ploots", "boxie ships" and "paper boats".

These consisted of, in turn, small wooden single plank shaped models with single mast, card sail and piece of thin metal as a keel and able to sail downwind only, modified fish boxes or other suitable crates converted to represent fishing boats complete with small pieces of herring nets, (daisies were herring, buttercups were codlings), and single-trip paper folded craft with paper sail and a few grains of shingle for ballast.

Even the large National Dried Milk metal tins provided material for models, opened up and beaten flat they could be shaped into a crude craft, with the seams at bow and stern folded over and hammered to provide a watertight joint. Carrying capacity was measured in how many whelks they could carry. Always handy with his hands it was Davie Fullerton who made the first prototype.

Other major activities for boys centred mostly on football and rounders, a form of baseball. With another school pal, Hance Fullerton, I seemed to spend hours kicking a football, either with organised "sides" during school dinner and playtime periods or "three goals and in". This was just the two of us with one shooting in at a goal formed by stone or jacket markers – score three goals and you were next in goal, the routine being repeated.

After finding an old and torn set of boxing gloves which previously had belonged to an uncle this provided another novel outlet for our boyish enthusiasm and energy. Before the days of computers and video games our boyhood was marked by an almost never-ending succession of outdoor and active pursuits during the daylight hours. In saying that, such chores as carrying two pails of water from the well or fetching a canister of milk from a nearby croft was normally fitted in after school.

At that time, with no mains water, the source was from natural springs. If lucky some were close by, when they were dry in the summer others still useable often involved up to half a mile trek. In times of real drought they were locked and only available twice a day. Some had hand-crank pumps which usually required priming if the level was very low, the more basic wells involved just lifting a lid and dropping a bucket into the open well and pulling up to tip into another. For drinking purposes this was usually an enamelled pail.

It was much easier to carry two loaded pails than one, made even easier by the use of a frame which kept them from banging against your knees and consequently spilling half the water. These wells were fed purely from natural springs, usually at the bottom of a hill, and as such no cleansing or other additives were injected but I cannot recall any readily identifiable maladies ensuing from its consumption.

My father on HMS *Shiant* in the Second World War.

In a small village the influence of family and friends was all round and many tasks were undertaken on a communal basis.

Early schooldays were in what was known as the "peerie room" at Hamnavoe School, with small desks with hinged lids, a hole for an inkwell, which I never ever saw used, and a slate to write on. My first teacher was Jemima Smith, later

My painting of HMS *Shiant* T170.

Walterson, who after a few months moved me up a class. I think the fact that I could read, write and spell quite well due to my mother instructing me daily prior to starting school, and that I was an avid reader, had something to do with it.

The downside was that I struggled with arithmetic, or sums as we called it then, so much so that when my mother saw I was having difficulty in keeping up with the older second-year classmates she asked the teacher to put me back with the first year pupils. She refused, on the grounds that she felt I would soon catch up, but this particular difficulty is something that has stayed with me. I never had any bother with algebra or geometry, and later calculus, but "sums" was always a sticking point and it was only because of my better exam results in the other subjects that kept me in the first five of my class in later years in secondary school. Similarly, the maths as applied to such subjects as heat engines, physics, mechanics and science in my later marine engineering certificate exams caused me no difficulty.

My Ward grandparents house at Houss. It had a thatched roof; the plastered gable end was an extension on the east side built later.

It was my mother who was undertook all the home tuition in these early days as my father had been called up to serve in the Royal Navy soon after I started school. Following a precedent set by my grandfather, having being a member of the Royal Naval Reserve and later Royal Navy in the First World War, it was almost a formality that my father would be conscripted into the Royal Navy having served in the RNR also. Such was the case, and in 1941, and being away for what a seemed an eternity with infrequent leave due to postings abroad, it was from my grandfather that I received much guidance and help in these formative years.

My mother had to supplement the meagre forces pay with hand knitting for sale and be very careful with outgoings. In this she was not unique as in common with most women of that era in the village she always seemed to be working or doing something productive. I do not think I ever saw her sitting doing nothing, and with no mains water or electricity normal household chores were much more labour intensive and time consuming than today.

My day started with her giving me a tablespoonful of raw cod liver oil and a beaten raw egg; I'm not sure which held the most terrors. Next, when I was at school, was checking each morning I had washed behind my ears and that under my fingernails were clean. In the evening it was homework, especially stressing reading and spelling.

Stoic to a fault, I only saw her in tears twice in my life; the first was when we received news that my father's ship, HMS *Shiant* was being sent abroad out of home waters, in this case the Mediterranean and, much later, when her youngest brother was lost by drowning.

If not in our house it was helping with the manual labour associated with the harvest cycle at my grandparents', Ward's, croft at Houss, at the other end of the island.

They lived in a thatched-roofed cottage comprising but end, ben end and a small closet with top and bottom bunk beds. There was no toilet; your business was conducted in the byre. I came to dread this operation in wintertime with darkness and a couple of cows for company. They had quite a lot of land cultivated, two long rigs on each side of the road leading up to Houss proper. Later an extension was built out at the front with wash basin and much later a stone-walled small enclosure with toilet in the adjoining yard. Thirteen of a family were brought up there, including twins, accommodated in this meagre accommodation only because the elders gradually moved out as the next were born and grew up.

The internal walls had bare whitewashed stone walls with very small windows, and an open loft stuffed with herring nets. Furnishing was equally basic, a dresser with crockery and cutlery, wooden armchair at the side of the fire in which my grandfather sat, and a long wooden backed bench, somewhat optimistically called the restin-shair, and a table. My grandfather Johnnie Ward was a tall man, in contrast my grandmother Elizabeth was quite small and a build to match, but believe you me when she said jump you immediately obeyed! My enduring memory of her is of a diminutive figure, habitually dressed in a black hap with grey hear in thick plaits.

Aunt Mary used to do the kirning in the front porch and after much pleading I was sometimes allowed to try, my enthusiasm was always exemplified and spoiled by a final forceful downward push which resulted in the contents being splashed all over the place, and being rewarded by a clip on the ear!

All the delling and harvesting seemed to be done by the women folk, the men being at the fishing. I can vividly remember Mary being harnessed to a large frame with downward protruding spikes dragging up and down the rigs to harrow and break up the surface.

Grannies Pottinger and Ward with our son Jim.

SCHOOL DAYS

School was a primary with only two rooms, the big room for the over ten-year-olds, and the peerie room for the younger pupils, with one teacher in each. Thus each teacher taught the varying age groups without any segregation, not ideal perhaps, but it did not seem to be any bar to anyone intending to go on to higher education.

Indiscipline was often corrected by either a wooden ruler or leather strap on the palm, not considered correct today perhaps but it never did any of us any harm and was definitely preferable to being "kept in" after end of period to write lines thus missing out on football or playing with boats.

One amusing episode, but not for the perpetrator or the rest of the class, was a trick played on the head teacher, Mr Johnston, who frequently went out in the boys' playground for a smoke in the afternoon. One of the Leask boys who sat in a seat just under the clock used to climb up on the seat and using a twelve-inch ruler pushed the minute hand on ten minutes. This went on several times until the teacher, suspecting some mischief, pulled a seat under the window outside and standing on it was able to spot the miscreant up to his dastardly deeds. The result being that we all had to stay an extra ten minutes for the rest of the week, the culprit was understandably not popular.

I am not sure of its provenance but I heard a tale that in one instance the hour hand instead of the minute had been moved on, with embarrassing results. Confessing to our parents to having been thus disciplined inevitably led to further retribution, and was possibly an even more effective deterrent.

Incredible as it seems now, with no local policeman on the

island, the head teacher would often take it on himself to punish any pupil acknowledged as being guilty of committing any act of vandalism, or annoyance to anyone in the village, albeit always of a minor and non-destructive nature, outwith school hours! Imagine that now!

That Mr Johnston had reportedly, whether true or not, suffered from some kind of shell shock during the First World War and he certainly displayed some rather erratic behaviour. When in the big room on one occasion when I was sharing a desk with Daisy Jamieson he apparently saw somebody misbehaving in the same row behind us and tore down the aisle with an outstretched pointer which, as he passed me, caught me just above my left eyebrow resulting in a fair sized gash when bled profusely. He obviously got such a fright that when he was upbraided by Daisy in no certain terms, which we all anticipated would result in some disciplinary response, he rather sheepishly turned away. I cannot recall any repercussions when I told my parents, but he left me with the legacy in that the hair of my eyebrow still fails to grow on that spot!

Norman Sutherland followed Mr Johnston, and was an entirely different sort. At that time there was a Fraser Cup presented at the annual sports held between Hamnavoe and Scalloway schools. Initially the winner was that with most points in the athletic sports over the event. Given the disparity in numbers it was, for reasons of fairness, decided that the cup would be decided by a relay race, with three in each team.

The Hamnavoe team won all the annual events I can recall, the main reason was that we had Rosabell Fullerton running the anchor leg and seemingly no matter how much ground she had to make up she always finished first.

This event had a surprising finale one year when we were all travelling back to Hamnavoe from Scalloway with the cup in one of the shop boats when we met a fishing boat coming in just past the Green Holm, they came close to us and enquired how we got on, for confirmation of our success Norman vigorously waved the cup aloft with such abandon that the top flew off and over the side!

As the cup had been won in a previous year it was always proudly displayed on the mantelpiece in the big room and had been the subject of a drawing exam, obviously he was happy with the realism of my drawing and sent it away to order a replica top for the cup.

Whilst I was still at the Hamnavoe school the local post office got word that the Danish cable ship *Eduard Suenson* was coming to do some work on the telephone cable in the area off Burwick, and that they required someone to act as pilot to guide in their arrival and when working around in this fairly congested area. Johnny Halcrow from the shop came and asked my father if he would go with the motor boat *Sylvanus* LK171 to guide the vessel.

I went with them and we met the cable ship out to the west and proceeded to lead the way to the area where she would be working. However, they obviously thought that it would be preferable to have the pilot on the bridge as they manoeuvred around inside and outside Langa so we went alongside and my father joined the cable ship. Somewhat to my surprise Johnny also went aboard leaving me in charge of the *Sylvanus*.

I would have been about ten or eleven years old at the time and was instructed to dodge about clear of the cable ship. Knowing that I would never be able to restart the engine unaided if it stopped I kept engine throttle a bit more open than a normal idling speed, with the resultant increased plume of white smoke. After a few hours when they beckoned me alongside the gangway the crew were somewhat surprised to see a young boy in short trousers coming out of the wheelhouse after I manoeuvred the *Sylvanus* alongside the gangway! After tying up we were all taken into the saloon to have a slap-up meal. In addition to the pilotage fee I think the ship's bond was a bit lighter when we left.

Soon came the eleven plus, or control test, as it was termed in these days. This was the great divider between those who were deemed capable, or had the urge, to go on to further education at either of the junior or senior secondary schools at Lerwick, and those who would finish their schooling in the local primaries. Because I was in a class above my age group the teacher had me doing a dummy run of the control test exam a year early.

The Central Public School could award a junior leaving certificate after three years' study, but the Anderson Educational Institute was able to teach to a standard such as to be able to award highers, and anyone with these sufficient qualifications, after completing six years, could be candidates for entrance to university.

As in most formal exams the result was often dictated by ability to pass the test on the day and you stood or fell accordingly, at that time when assessments were not in vogue it was the only measure of ability then deemed applicable.

I think the examination paper was a standard one for Orkney and Shetland and, to my surprise, I was awarded a book by The Orkney and Shetland Association examination prizes in recognition of my efforts, a very small volume, *The Heroes*, describing some of the exploits in Greek Mythology. This was in confirmation of achieving a standard which allowed me the choice of which further educational establishment I preferred.

Why did I choose the Central instead of the Institute? To this day I am not sure why I made the choice, inevitably and unconsciously ships and a marine environment had to figure somewhere in the future scheme of things. Perhaps it was because I felt that six years was too long cooped up, it may even be because I felt in some way that my parents would find it difficult to support me through this extended period, though I am sure that in common with many others in the same situation mine would always be prepared to make the necessary sacrifice.

More plausibly, it was because I did not have the benefit of any career adviser to point out the advantages of a more academic background to support my ultimate preferred direction.

Despite gaining the qualifications to attend the Anderson Institute, I dropped the opportunity to enter into a senior secondary education and enrolled at the Central in late summer of 1948.

I was 11 years of age when my brother Drewy was born. Shortly afterwards I went to secondary school in Lerwick and was only home at weekends in the summer and holidays. Thus we had limited time together in our childhood.

My first lodgings were with Magnus Leask and family at South Setter, Gulberwick, who were very homely and caring, the only down side was that it was a fair buks knee-deep in heather, or snow, from the house up to the main road to catch the school bus. Due to the *Tirrick* ferry not running late in the afternoon in winter it was not possible to get home at the weekends at all, and in summer after a weekend home at Hamnavoe, Hyndy Johnston's bus, which ran from Scalloway to Lerwick on Sunday night, used to drop me off at the Hollanders Knowe to foot it to South Setter. Apart from once when a policeman in a passing Black Maria stopped and gave me a lift! The last lesson period on Fridays was in the gym under Mr Bennet. If he had allowed me off a bit earlier I could have caught the bus to Scalloway and the ferry to Hamnavoe, no such luck however.

I stayed at Gulberwick from August in the first year until the following April, 1949, when I moved to stay with my aunt Ruby and uncle Arthur Sinclair when they got a Cruden house in Meadowfield Road in Scalloway, several Burra families took up residence in these houses at that time.

It was when I was about 13 years old that I decided to build a canoe, or kayak as is now termed, something completely new in the village. I drew out the various shapes in the technical drawing class at secondary school and from these sketches formed the various frames, laboriously hand sawing out the long full-length thin laths to just over quarter of an inch thick to support the covering skin from a two-inch thick plank; it was only later on a visit to Moores in Scalloway, and discussing my project with Cecil Duncan, that he kindly arranged to

I built this canoe when I was at school, covered it with flour bags from Mowat's bakery at Scalloway and well coated it to make her watertight.

have the remainder of the strips ripped out on their power saw. I then loaded our small boat with long timber deals and motored the few miles across to the mainland, and within minutes I had available what had taken me days of hard labour to accomplish. Not having any canvas for covering the canoe I resorted to using three flour bags bought from Mowats the Scalloway baker, shaped and treating these with a mixture of linseed and paint rendered them watertight.

My parents, and grandmother especially, had done their best to dissuade me from what seemed a foolhardy adventure, "boy you will make your end in it" but seeing I was not to be deflected she accepted the inevitable but was determined that things were done right, and sewed the bags roughly to shape on her Singer sewing machine. This came naturally to her as her father had been a noted sail maker for small Shetland type boats during her childhood.

This strange craft was to be a source of much comment and curiosity and afforded me many hours of pleasure during school holidays, experimenting with rudders, paddles and boards to act as a sail to travel downwind.

Secondary schooling went all too fast, the more outrageous acts of indiscipline were met with the strap, or lines or being "kept in", and if given the choice we all opted for the short sharp shock administered by the belt, by that time we were of equal height to many of the teachers. Looking back, we never gave much thought to the practice but now it does seem a bit ludicrous for someone to be hitting a grown boy on the hand bit a leather strap.

That said I have nothing but admiration for the teachers during my spell at the Central, who certainly did their best to be educational and stimulating. Discipline was ensured by a variety of methods, being greatly differed and influenced by the character and general demeanour of each teacher. As an example, Nancy Stewart was our English teacher, and as being a kindly person we never tried to take advantage of her, Nellie Smith taught arithmetic and one look from her was enough. T. A. Robertson, or "bappy" as he was nicknamed for some unknown reason, was subject to numerous childish pranks by our class, one would involve one of the boys in the back row of seats making a loud groaning noise, Bappy would storm down the aisle to administer a reprimand, on nearing the offender someone in the front row would replicate the noise, cue, the first offender claiming his innocence as it was obviously from some other source. This routine was sometimes played repeatedly until some of the girls in the class would pass the word along "that's enough". Even now I feel shame at subjecting such a nice well-meaning teacher who was dedicated to his profession and only wished the best for his pupils. He was a prolific contributor of poems and stories to *The New Shetlander* magazine under the pen name Vagaland, and I was gratified to get to know him better after leaving school when having a number of contributions published in this magazine.

I think my only contact with the headmaster, George W. Blance, known as Dodie Willie, was in very unusual circumstances. His office was in the short corridor beside the door to the science room and I suppose in an effort to monitor the happenings there he had a clear panel in the frosted glass section of the science room door, and was known to have a peek in regularly.

On this occasion he apparently did so and then came into our room and to my surprise beckoned me out to his office. Once there he then questioned me "were you behaving yourself?" he demanded. Being completely innocent of any perceived misdemeanour I replied "yes, I was". He then repeated his original question to which I gave the same answer, noting that he had now taken the strap out of drawer in his desk.

After third such duet I said, " If you are going to give me the strap then do it, as you are going to get the same answer". As a third-year pupil and as big as he was the strap really did not have any terrors.

He duly gave me three of the best and told me to get back to my class, where on entering the science teacher, Lowrie Johnston, asked what it was all that about. On hearing my explanation he said "but I don't think you were misbehaving" and immediately made tracks to Dodie's office. On his return he came over and said "I've sorted that out, now forget all about it". Back then I suppose getting the strap was a fact of life, but thinking back now it does seem ludicrous for an adult to be belting a youth with a leather strap in the confines of a school, something that today would be a criminal offence.

As a digression, on a visit back to Shetland in 2009 a happy reunion for classmates was arranged to be held in a local hotel, sadly, and inevitably, the available numbers were understandably much reduced.

During the school holidays one break coincided with the coming of mains electricity to Burra and, with Ronnie and Billy Goodlad, and Jim Henry, got a job digging the holes for the cable transmission poles, six feet deep by six feet long. On naturally querying why six feet long, the answer was, try and swing a pick at the bottom of the hole with anything less!

All the poles had to be in a dead straight line, inevitably a big rock would be in the way at some locations, no power tools at all were available and in some cases a hole was hand chipped out deep enough to insert a small dynamite charge. However, this was not advisable if in close proximity to a house when there was nothing for it but to hack away with a cold chisel. I still recall one unfortunate encounter with such an obstacle right outside the northwest corner of the front garden wall of Ollie Goodlad's house.

Seeing my predicament one of the men, a Mr Jamieson of Sandwick, who at the time had a daughter Elma in the same class year as me at the Central, took pity and got the foreman to arrange to set a small charge to shatter the unforgiving rock, Ollie taking a particular interest to ensure plenty of deadening material was being placed on top of the charge.

If I recall correctly us younger trio were getting about one shilling an hour, Billy being older got halfway between that and the men's rate, that is until we protested that we were digging the same size holes and should be rewarded accordingly, a plea that was in fact rewarded with an increase.

LEAVING SCHOOL

After I left school I got a job with Willie Goodlad, known better as Willie o' Blomers, who had a small building business in Burra. First jobs included loading a cement mixer and other labouring jobs, but being reasonably handy with tools I was soon put on house extensions doing joinery jobs, mainly lining block walls and fitting plasterboard, hanging doors and fitting skirting boards and door facings, similar jobs to those being done by journeymen. Cheap labour I suppose one would call it but a welcome step up from general labouring.

At that time building regulations were much more relaxed than now. In contrast to current practice the inside of the concrete block walls were merely strapped and plasterboard nailed on without any insulation whatsoever. Having some aptitude for drawing I was then tasked by Willie with drawing four identical copies in the evening, no copiers then, of any planned extension or alteration he was about to undertake for a customer, to be submitted to the local authority. Each was laboriously drawn with a common pen nib and ink on plain paper, new additions marked in red, an effort which I was remunerated by, I think, £4 for each set.

My ambitions were probably somewhat different to what was on offer, and I looked to a possible career in design and draughtsmanship in mechanical engineering. But I will always be grateful for the spell working for Willie as I was to gain experience with working with adults and mostly unsupervised.

It was thus that my next step was to be interviewed by the local education authority in the person of Mr J. W. Irvine, and accepted in a scheme operated by the Highlands and Islands to subsidise lodging fees to allow candidates to undergo apprenticeships or other training in the south.

At that time the economy of Shetland was in a condition far removed from having the bounty of any oil revenue, and the fishing industry was a barely providing a living, and I was only one of many boys and girls who took the route south to hopefully gain an apprenticeship, nursing training, or other qualification to better their prospects.

A MARINE ENGINEERING APPRENTICESHIP IN THE 1950s

Training in shipbuilding and engineering was available at a number of centres, including the nearest at Aberdeen but eschewing the close proximity of this city with the obvious possible temptation of wanting to take the next ferry home, the Clyde seemed to be the obvious choice.

In my eyes Glasgow was too big, so the choice was Greenock, a choice possibly made only by sticking a pin on the map. Luckily this led me to Scotts' Shipbuilding & Engineering Company Ltd., a well-known and respected establishment at Greenock.

Passage to Aberdeen from Lerwick was on the venerable MV *St Ninian*. As one could imagine it was something of a shock for a 15-year old to be sent from Shetland to arrive in Aberdeen on the mainland of Scotland, never having seen a train, or even a proper tree come to think of it. Train journey was Aberdeen to Glasgow Queen Street Station, hoof it down to Central Station, and another train to Greenock.

Duly arriving at Greenock in November 1951 on a miserable dark night, only partly alleviated by the horrible orange glow of sodium streetlights, I found that my lodgings were within a flat about 15 minutes' walk from Scotts'. Luck was certainly on my side here, as I was to spend all of nearly five years with Mr and Mrs Lowrie, and a more respectable and caring couple it would have been hard to find.

I was fortunate, as later experience confirmed, to gain an apprenticeship with the well respected and long established Scotts' Shipbuilding & Engineering Company Ltd. at Greenock to give its rightful full title, indeed the same Scott family connection could be traced back to 1711, though oddly enough the company's full address was still via Greenock Foundry, harking back to earlier days.

At that time it was customary for many boys in the interim between leaving school at 15 and reaching the required age of 16 to start a full apprenticeship to be employed in various departments in a very junior position, such as store boys, helpers in the time and bonus offices and other such lowly stations.

As noted above my own entry into this new world was somewhat different, at that time there was a scheme whereby pupils from the Scottish Highland and Islands could be awarded what amounted to a scholarship after the interview by local director of education in that a subsidy was paid to cover lodgings and minimal pocket money until wages reached £5. This bounty, minimal as it was, opened a route to qualifications and a trade possibly not previously available to many. It was paid every Friday at close of work and by calling at the local labour exchange on my way to my lodgings and presenting my pay slip, whereupon they did the necessary calculation to make up the difference due for my lodgings.

The more I earned in the small increases for each year served had the effect of reducing my allowance from them. Whilst this gratuity was welcome it was somewhat depressing to have my weekly allowance reduced by any excess earned over that figure due to bonus or overtime!

One journeyman I worked with in particular took great umbrage with this arrangement and often pleaded on my behalf, without success I may add. It was for this reason that contrary to many I naturally refused to work overtime or on nightshift during my apprenticeship, much to the astonishment of my colleagues.

With only a few days after arrival in the town before reaching the required age I was soon inducted into the somewhat testing experience of the engineering training department, with its tribal customs in all its forms, a ritual which I am sure was repeated throughout the similar establishments around the UK. All of which in my own case epitomised the stark contrast between Greenock and a small fishing village in Shetland.

It was in fact a culture shock writ large, and there were various degrees of initiation to undergo and experience until your status in the pecking order was established. The first usually involved a ducking by being lifted bodily and dumped in the large deep hand washing trough, I avoided this unwelcome bath by stating that it was OK by me but be aware that one at least of the perpetrators would be joining me in the bath.

Another trick was to set light to any cleaning rag stuffed in the back pocket of your boiler suit, next was to put a bolt through the button-holes of your jacket and rivet it over the head of a nut. There was no official tea break in the mornings but you had a special heavy thick rimmed metal can which could be filled with boiling water from a boiler geyser heated at an open furnace at set times.

Almost always the residue of tea leaves and hot water would be tossed over any unsuspecting boy, I was the recipient of this once, and naturally chased the miscreant with my own can to give him same treatment until we reached a dead end in the workshop. Panicking as I reached him he then threw the heavy can at me which cut open my forehead which bled profusely. Unknown to both of us the training instructor had actually seen what happened and sent me to the ambulance room where I had to have several stitches inserted. In answer to the query by the nurse as to how it happened I just said that I had banged my head on a drilling machine.

On going back to the training school the instructor took us both to the personnel manager, who was responsible for the administration of the apprentices, and informed him what had really happened. Just with that the works nurse came in to report the claimed accident and naturally, given my somewhat edited version of the events to her earlier, she was a little surprised to learn the true facts. The personnel manager had no doubt seen it all before, and remarked that omerta was sometimes best in the circumstances and waved me away, but not before suspending the offender for a fortnight without pay. Back in the training centre I was a hero not having "clyped" on the miscreant. It was your conduct in such things that smoothed one's rite of passage in an environment which has to be said would not be tolerated today.

As a marine engineer apprentice with Scotts' Shipbuilding & Engineering Co. in Greenock.

As can be gathered it was a rough school, one episode will illustrate the daily hazards. One of the lads for no reason threw a heavy iron bar which hit a fellow apprentice who was operating a lathe in the ankle. It hit with such force that he passed out, whereupon the perpetrator then shoved the victim, still comatose, under the machine in an effort of concealment. To add insult to injury the training instructor, assuming the poor lad was larking and malingering as usual, started prodding him and ordering him to get up and stop carrying on!

This, and other initiation rites, was too much for a lad from Skye who started at the same time as me and he decided to give it all a miss and return home. I also had some doubts at times, but I suppose the fact that there was so to speak an investment made in my career and the feeling that I would be letting down my parents hopes, made me stick with it, plus the fact that I was determined to give as good as I got. Oddly enough I can remember the names of almost all the apprentices, and further down the line all the journeymen engineers I later worked with as an apprentice nearly seventy years ago.

Whilst I would defend Scotts' to anyone, I felt that progress through the various departments of the engine works to gain experience was largely due your own initiative, and even given the fairly long periods I spent in each department my request for a change was almost inevitably met with the comment by the respective managers "you are always wanting a move to somewhere else".

The first nine months was spent in the training centre, and then out in the big wide world of the large engine works, at that time large marine diesels and steam turbines and associated items were being manufactured in-house, with boilers and the myriad of associated items of pipework, ducting and pattern making in adjacent buildings. At that time Scotts' could manufacture a complete engine room and related items with minimal subcontracting out, as well as building a wide variety of naval surface warships and submarines and merchant vessels. The shipyard proper was on the Clyde seafront across the main street from the engine works.

My five years were spent roughly as follows: Nine months in apprentice training school; one year in engine shops and marking off table; one year on overhaul and conversion of submarines in shipyard outfitting basin and drydock; one year on installation of machinery on Leopard class frigate HMS *Puma* in shipyard basin; one year on installation of turbine and boiler machinery on merchant ships in shipyard basin and the last three months on close-fitting in machine shops.

The company had a long pedigree in the construction of all types or merchant ships, sail and power, and for the Admiralty from the biggest to the smallest, including submarines, and it is sobering to compare a view of the shipyard site when it was demolished to that in its heyday.

At that time many of the older employees had worked on some of the warships built by Scotts' that had outstanding records in service in the Second World War, and there was a definite, and deserved, pride in knowing that they individually contributed to their success, and equally some sadness in knowing that many did not survive the conflict.

As is well known there was, and still is to a degree, divisions between the Catholic and Protestant religions in the west of Scotland, something that was then completely alien to me. My first experience of this was being questioned as to what school I had attended. This was because the name Pottinger had no religious connotations, that of Patrick, Boyle, Donnachie, in some instances for example, but not exclusively, were usually used by Catholics. For the life of me I could not fathom what interest the school I went to would be to anyone. It was only when I enquired from my landlady the import of the query, for instance if I had attended such schools as St Mary's or St Joseph's then my religion would have been pretty well defined.

Now in the picture I really hammed it up by saying that I had attended the correctly identified establishment Lerwick Central Public School, emphasis being on the Public!

A response that created some wonderment as you can well imagine! I experienced this odd attitude on several occasions later when being quite friendly with some Catholic workmates I was often asked "do you know they were Catholics, but you are not a Catholic" my response always was that I could not care less, they were good pals and that was good enough for me.

Amusing now but not then was when I was working on a submarine in our own drydock. The task entailed me crouching in one of the torpedo tube exterior openings in the casing holding a steel straight edge to allow the journeyman inside I was working with to check the travel of one of the torpedo tube cap doors. In such a position the back of my neck was hard up under a cut-out in the plate above and unbeknown to me a painter was working in the space above. His presence was soon made obvious when I felt the swish of a big paint brush across the back of my neck! I am not sure who got the biggest fright, I or him when I unexpectedly crawled out to confront him as he was completely unaware that I was working below him.

It was during my spell on the HMS *Puma*, a Type 41 frigate heavily armed with two pairs of 4.5ins guns, when she was outfitting in the dock basin that the journeymen went on strike. At that time I was one of the senior apprentices so I was detailed with a younger lad to carry on lining up the propeller shaft bearings and supporting pads, which were individually hand scraped to ensure a close fit between the underside of the bearings and the top of the mounting stools.

The three engine rooms took up about 30% of the length of the ship with four main diesel engines geared to each propeller shaft and four diesel generators installed in echelon. Given the flexibility of the after part of the hull, exacerbated by the wash generated by ships passing up and down the Clyde a short distance from the mouth of the fitting-out basin where we were berthed, it was quite difficult to achieve the necessary fit.

As I recall the limit of tolerance of difference over the surface of the steel pads between the fitting parts was 1½ thousands of an inch, and it did not matter how often I achieved this fit the foreman always got a different reading. I was so certain of my reading on my occasion that with some indignation I called him back to check his figures, after trials with his feelers his response was the classic: "Maybe my feeler gauge is a bit more worn than yours!" I was never sure if he was trying me on or not.

As noted above the frigate had three engine rooms and there was some red faces all round when it was found that a large gearwheel had been placed in the wrong engine room much earlier, and as it was too big to pass through the hatches a hole had to be cut in one engine room deck to lift it out another in the adjacent one to lower it in.

It may not come as a surprise to many readers that the facilities and amenities down in the shipyard, as apart from the offices, were somewhat basic, there was only one building with about half a dozen washbasins and toilet cubicles for the thousands of employees, wash basin plugs and door locks were something of a novelty. In fact the above facility was a recent addition, previously the toilets consisted of sitting on a long plank with half-height divisions above a water-fed trough at a slight angle running the full length, all of which projected out over the dockside above the water, no problems with lack of flush or blocked pipes here. In practice it did work, although you had not survived a rite of passage until you had the unfortunate experience of getting a slightly warm posterior caused by someone at the high end setting afloat a burning newspaper which naturally floated merrily downstream!

Any poor lad who was about to enter into matrimony was naturally fair game for a doing, in one case it may have had an outcome not envisaged. The shipyard had a large steel box about four feet square with three sides and open at one end and top with wire lifting slings which was used for lifting a variety of pipes, valves and fittings aboard any ship alongside in the fitting-out basin with one of the large overhead cranes which could span the full width of the basin. This unfortunate was duly trussed hand and foot and put in one of these boxes and swung out and then lowered down to just above the surface of the water. Being close to the side wall of the basin it was impossible see it unless standing at the edge.

There may have been some queries by foremen or managers curious as to why this box was in this position, it having been swung so the open end was nearly up against the opposite side of the basin wall thus hiding the contents, it was rumoured that someone had offered the reasonable explanation that the craneman had lowered it so as to visually check the full length of the crane wires! Inevitably the perpetrators forgot about their prank and it was only discovered when a passer-by heard the shouts and investigated where they were emanating from. Not only had he been forgotten about it was also forgotten that the tide had risen in the interim and was lapping over the open side of the box!

Nobody owned up in the inevitable subsequent investigation and all kept stum, and as fortunately no real harm was done it was taken as an example, albeit somewhat extreme, of practices often perpetuated on a prospective groom.

For a while in winter I was suffering from repeated sore throats, so in the end I was sent to a local hospital to have my tonsils removed, coincidentally the date of the operation was my 18th birthday. There must have been some complications as I was kept in for two weeks after the procedure. By this time the nurses were wondering why I never had any visitors and on hearing of my particular circumstances and the date of my birthday they gave me small iced cake and they took it on themselves to give me special care and attention. As can be expected, at that age I had a good appetite and soon being well on the mend the night shift nurses when having their main meal used to waken me and bring a plateful.

At that time a bus trip for a winter weekend at Blackpool was a popular event, and one of the men in Scotts' used to make all the arrangements and each week he collected a small amount for a kitty to pay for the bus and accommodation. Normally he would have made a trip earlier to check the accommodation but for some reason he had not done so in this instance, with unfortunate results.

Five of us apprentices were in a room, basically in the loft, accessed by a ladder and then a hole cut in a partition, three to one bed and two in the other, sleeping arrangements were rotated on the toss of coin. The space was so cramped that when one of us stood up to get dressed the others had to lie on the bed. On our way downstairs we would pass an open door to a bathroom which, believe it or not, had a bed frame and bedding placed on top of the bath!

The lady of the house did the cooking and mine host served the breakfast, the presentation of which was somewhat novel to say the least in that on occasion he carried food with one hand and a cat under his other arm.

In our party were a number of bus conductresses from Greenock, as a rule not known for taking any prisoners, amply demonstrated when the man of the house dropped a spoon on to the floor, picked it up and causally wiped it under his armpit. Let's just say he was rather forcibly advised as to where he could put this cutlery item!

The Blackpool Winter Garden dance hall where the music was provided by Jack Parnell and his band was a popular venue with such huge crowds that it was a struggle to get on the dance floor. One of our group had bought a new pair of flannel trousers of which he seemed inordinately proud, however this pride was somewhat dented when a prone reveller was being carried out rather worse for wear and, as he neared our pal, turned his head to the side and vomited all over the new breeks. We visited the famous Tower Ballroom which somewhere in the building had a large parrot in a cage, one of our group frustrated by its seemingly inability to talk punched the side of the cage with the result that the bird dropped down seemingly comatose or worse – shades of John Cleese's parrot sketch! Cue a hasty retreat by all concerned.

This is how us young blades used to dress on a Saturday afternoon when parading along the main street in Greenock, no anoraks and jeans then! With two fellow marine engineer apprentices.

Looking at photos taken in the 1950s and 60s showing people walking along the main street of Greenock it is noticeable that unless in working clothes all the pedestrians were, so to speak, formally dressed. The men and youths all had shirt and ties and females coats or dresses. It was the done thing for youths "going down the town" to be smartly dressed with polished shoes. I remember at one stage it was de rigueur for us young blades to wear an overcoat, scarf and soft hat!

The apparent importance of sartorial excellence in that era was exemplified when after a few dates with a one girl she remarked that my socks did not match my coat. My criteria was only that hopefully they matched each other. Truth to tell we were both looking for an excuse to terminate the relationship and this was a good excuse as any.

At that time the popular local hop was the long-gone and much loved Cragburn dance hall at Gourock. Here Henri Morrison and his Swingstars held sway with his excellent band, not to mention his wife and singer Bessie. They played there three or four nights every week and were the highlight of the week, especially on Saturday, where largely the same crowd attended. This meeting place over the years must have been responsible for a goodly number of marriages.

I had noticed a lovely dark-haired girl who, after her lunch, walked up the street from her home at the bottom of the street where I lodged to her work in the local Co-op offices which were more or less opposite my lodgings. After describing her to one of my fellow apprentices who was a regular at Cragburn he told me her name was Ruby MacDonald and that they had been in same class at school at one time. He said she went to Cragburn every Saturday night and his advice was to join him there next Saturday which would be my chance to get to know her.

Nothing daunted I took his advice but every time I made an approach to her to ask her to dance someone would always beat me to it. In the end I grabbed my opportunity – as chance would have it was a quickstep! At that time my terpsichorean abilities were pretty basic. Not surprisingly she often later said she still had the scars to prove it!

The band took an interval halfway through the session and this was the chance to invite your fancy to join you to take a soft drink up the balcony during this break (imagine, a dance hall with no alcohol, oh how innocent it all was then!) It was reckoned that if you had got this far then your chances were quite good from then on, possibly leading to accompanying them home at the end of the dance.

Whilst overtures on first dates are sometimes rather tentative something must have clicked as this was the start of a courtship resulting in almost 57 years of a very happy marriage until sadly my Ruby was taken away.

FIRST SHIP IN MERCHANT NAVY

With my engineering apprenticeship completed the options were two years national service, a duty which was deferred whilst an apprentice, and joining the merchant navy provided you stayed until the age of 26.

It therefore seemed that the choice between advancing one's career and being reasonably well paid and cared for, or as a lowly conscript being shouted at by a sergeant, or worse, for 24 months was indeed a no brainer.

In the middle 1950s all the shipping companies were re-establishing their traditional trade routes and rebuilding and augmenting their fleets after the depredations of the war, and as such we could have our choice of berths. Such was the need for marine engineers that my employers were willing to grant my full apprenticeship certificate three months early if I joined the British India Company who were currently having two cargo liners built by the company. However, now with a regular girlfriend it seemed preferable to join a company based at Glasgow and having regular sailings from the Clyde.

Whilst deck officers on joining the merchant navy had the benefit of some appropriate pre-sea training in one of the preparatory establishments, marine engineers were more likely to be pitched aboard often having served an apprenticeship of a type and environment far divorced from that likely to be encountered on board ship.

The British India Steam Navigation Company was an umbrella organisation which included a wide variety of interests and, whilst the name suggested a concentration on the Indian sub-continent, in fact the company encompassed a number of areas of the antipodes, Middle and Far East.

To satisfy the multifarious cargo and passenger requirements of these diverse trade routes a large variety of types of ships of all sizes was employed in the fleet. Whilst the majority were built in Britain the majority would never return to these shores, except in very few instances where they came back for scrapping.

Manning of officers could be a problem on these ships. The standard term of engagement on signing on was two-and-half years which could sometimes mean regular leave after a relatively short time measured in months when sailing on the direct UK-Australia-New Zealand routes for example. It could also equally result in a transfer to vessels trading exclusively on the Indian based routes for the duration of the statutory contract.

This long spell abroad obviously did not suit many, so officers sailing on the Eastern route often tended to serve for one "spell" only, or alternatively, there were those who in common parlance "went native", often having permanent liaisons with Oriental members of the fair sex which offered an attraction to stay permanently on the Indian coast or on Far East trades.

The end of my five-year apprenticeship coincided with the completion of the British India cargo liner *Nowshera*, on which I had spent a considerable time on the manufacture and installation of the propelling machinery, including an earlier spell measuring up the ship's turbine casings on the engine works surface marking-off table.

A short explanation might help here for it was really a proving exercise. Raw castings and forgings were set up on a large level steel table, and we had to mark off the main cutting lines on these using the machining drawings to ensure the various contours and shapes would in fact allow machining to the finished profiles etc.

The standby chief engineer and other senior engineers were naturally keen to recruit people with background knowledge of the installation, albeit as a first tripper, and encouraged me to apply for entrance to the company.

My application to the London office was duly acknowledged, with an enclosed railway warrant to proceed to Skelmorlie station, over the Renfrewshire border in Ayrshire. As the upper Greenock railway line terminated at Wemyss Bay, some distance short of Skelmorlie, which in fact was not connected by a railway, I opted to take a bus instead!

Duly presenting myself to the address in a nice bungalow, sited high above the coastal road with an enviable view of river traffic on the broad reaches of the lower Clyde, I was interviewed by the retired chief engineer officer of the company. Mr J. Caskies's conclusion was that I was a proper and suitable candidate for entry to the august B.I. company and approved to join the ship, which would be engaged on the UK-New Zealand-Australian route.

Concurrently with these discussions I was taking soundings with a number of ex-seagoing engineers in Scotts' who had experience of the company. They warned me of the possibility of being transferred to the Indian coast at any time despite signing on a ship on the regular UK outward route. Another factor to be considered was a burgeoning courtship with Ruby who, obviously and understandably, would not be keen on such a long separation. These considerations in the end led me to decline the offer and apply to Clan Line instead which offered the possibility of a regular call at nearby Glasgow.

As I recall my first stop was to the merchant navy establishment at the Broomilaw, then on to the Clan Line offices at Hope Street in Glasgow, who determined the suitability or otherwise of this raw entrant. Given the demand for bodies at this time it would be indeed be something of a calamity if one could not satisfy the most basic of requirements.

At that time Greenock had its own equivalent of Gieves, the well-known marine outfitters. Gilchrists could supply a made-to-measure doeskin uniform complete with the appropriate braid – Clan Line sporting their own curly-looped arm band instead of the usual diamond shaped embellishment.

With a successful interview and medical behind me, and

proudly decked out in doeskin uniform replete with the impressive Clan Line braid of single stripe with curly loop, I duly presented myself on the modern *Clan Maciness* at King George V dock at Glasgow as a junior engineer officer, a rank not even graced with a number to designate any pecking order. Just junior.

Coming up the gangway I was greeted by the second engineer with, "great, you can do all the nights!" Luckily only one diesel generator was running and an auxiliary Cochran boiler operating, so it was a case of watch and monitor only.

After a quick briefing of what valves to open and close, which temperatures to check, and – the most important instruction – to only call the duty senior engineer in a dire emergency, I was left on my own in the engine room from 1800 to 0600 hours. Needless to say I spent the whole twelve hours dashing around checking temperatures, pressures and water levels on the diesel generator and the boiler. Having been built as late as 1952 everything on board was bright and new, and I duly sounded out the possibility of a permanent posting aboard but alas all the roster had already been agreed for next voyage.

As we were lying in the line's regular berth in KGV dock my girlfriend caught the bus to Glasgow from Greenock which passed close to the head of the dock one Sunday to visit me, naturally running the gauntlet of all the onlookers on other ships as she walked down the dock to our ship. Clan Line being an enlightened management allowed a lowly junior and his girlfriend to have our lunch and evening meal in the main dining saloon with the rest of the officers.

Next ship to standby in Glasgow was in complete contrast, the war-built SS *Clan Urquart*. Apart from her twin screw triple expansion engines with Bauer Wach exhaust turbines and Scotch boilers, my only recall of this ship was the bare steel deck in my cabin.

This sojourn was to be brief, and soon I was instructed to make my way to West India Docks in London to join the TSS *Umgeni*. I was well aware that this could not be a Clan ship, but in fact

TSS *Umgeni*, my first ship in the merchant navy.

belonged to Bullard King, a Union Castle subsidiary, and now part of the Clan Line Union Castle British & Commonwealth conglomerate. But, being fed up with hanging around in port, I jumped at the chance to go deep sea.

Luckily I kept a diary of logging on times, dates of entry and departure and the various ship movements for all the ships I served on which is a revealing record of a type of seafaring now but a memory in the wake of container and bulk carriers.

With another first trip colleague I joined the ship at her usual berth at West Indian Dock in London on 22nd December, 1956, and a few days later we sailed to Hull, where we spent Christmas Day and the end of the year including New Year's Day, then across to Antwerp then Hamburg.

The Yorkshire ports, Hull and Middlesbrough, always seemed to be favourites for a run ashore for us young lads; the fair sex seemed to be most friendly. A few of us aboard the *Umgeni* decided to sample the delights of the Saturday dance at the Hull town hall and a good time was held by all.

It was noticeably warm inside and at one period I decided

to sit one dance out. It was then I happened to note a nice-looking girl already noted with approval by my shipmates standing nearby leaning against a pillar. Just then I saw that she seemed to be in some distress and started to slump against the column. Ever gallant what one could do but render assistance, fortunately she had nothing more serious wrong with her than she was feeling the heat and, after approaching her to see that she was OK, the least I could do was agree to her suggestion that I see her safely home. "You lucky beggar" was among the more polite comments from my colleagues when back at the ship. By contrast, as can well be imagined, the more revealing nocturnal displays exhibited at Antwerp, and especially Hamburg, were something of a shock to a first tripper.

The ship carried around 140 passengers and did the round trip starting at London, then Hull, Antwerp, Hamburg, London, then departing outward bound calling at Las Palmas, St Helena (to land a sick passenger), Capetown, Port Elizabeth, East London, Durban, Beira, Lourenco Marques, then same homeward via Durban, East London, Port Elizabeth, Capetown, Las Palmas and finally London. The complete deep sea voyage lasted from 23rd January to 28th March, 1957.

The passengers, some of whom did the round trip, but disembarking at Cape Town or Durban and rejoining when we were homeward bound, seemed a mixed crowd of middle age and older. Our description, whether true or not, was that they were rich Yorkshire mill owners, or guests of the company as payback for past outward freights, some were fairly well-to-do obviously, as many took their housemaids with them, their youth being a welcome diversion for us as would be noted later.

Down below in the engine room the ship left a lot to be desired and hopefully was not typical of the standard of the rest of the mighty Union Castle Line. The engineers' accommodation was primitive with a number of poky little cabins and us humble engineers were not allowed to eat in the main saloon with the passengers and deck officers but had to make do with a shabby messroom. We were, however, allowed up on an aft section of the upper deck at dances and social functions, but not at the cocktail bar.

We had the last laugh however as we had part refrigerated cargo stowed amidships and the temperature sounding pipes were located in the passenger cabin alleyways and had to be checked and recorded at regular intervals over the twenty four hours by the relevant watchkeeping junior engineer. Naturally this duty was eagerly anticipated by us juniors during the wee small hours as by this time we had sussed out which were adjacent to the maids' cabins. It was only later in the voyage that it was cottoned on to by the senior watchkeepers that for some reason this duty always took longer during the night watches than during the daylight hours!

My cabin was one of two situated in a small lobby off the main alleyway. The other was home to a South African engineer working his passage to the UK, he being notable for never appearing on time to start his watch, a definite no-no on any ship. The chief engineer had got wind of this, and had caught him still in his bunk on one occasion, so regularly used to check, his presence betrayed by the whiff of his cigar smoke.

Outward bound it was my misfortune to be the junior on watch with a certain fourth engineer. I will refer to him as N, who was the most miserable article I ever sailed with, whose prime objective was to emphasise his, minimal, place in the pecking order of seniority. Any supposed failure in carrying out one's delegated tasks was rewarded by the riposte that "I am a senior engineer and what I say goes, any cheek and I will take you up in front of the chief engineer officer"

The engine room of this ship when at sea had numerous leakages from piping and other steam connections which gradually filled up the bilges in the engine room which regularly had to be pumped out. It was taboo to operate the main steam-driven bilge pump to discharge this water as it would take steam away from that being supplied to the main engines. Instead we were ordered to use the notoriously ineffective engine-driven pumps.

During one watch I had religiously complied with this edict and after much coaching and priming of the pumps was patting myself on the back at having emptied all the water from the bilges, only to be confronted by our hero to the effect that he had done an inspection and the "bilges are full". I of course denied this and asked him to come and check. In reality it was only a small amount of water which was washing back and fore and across the tanktop with the movement of the ship that he was seeing, and not any depth of water in the bilge. His response was that "If I say the bilges are full of water they are full whether they are or not." Being a first tripper, and perhaps naïve in respect of what the penalties were for perceived dereliction of duty, I am afraid I had but to comply, however unjustified.

Homeward bound I buttonholed the second engineer and asked to be allocated to another watchkeeper as I was not going to put up with such childishness and pettiness – he gave me a knowing look he did as I had requested.

Homeward bound I got my revenge in spades when I was on watch with another senior. I still remember his name, Leslie Curwin, from Isle of Man. Practice at sea was to call the next watch at "one bell"; that is, the engine room bell was rung at 15 minutes before the end of the watch and a current watch keeper would then go up and wake the next watch so as they would get out of bed, if at night. They would then make their way down to the engine room for an initial inspection of the engine room and if all was in order accept responsibility and relieve the previous watch.

After four hours plus in a noisy and hot engine room it was a mark of respect and competence that the next watch would be prompt in relieving the previous watch. It so happened that the aforementioned character was especially prone to turn over in his bunk after being called despite several calls and on this occasion he overstepped the mark. His junior partner on his watch had already come down to the engine room to relieve me and my senior said, "That's now OK up you go Jim". It was some time later that N as Leslie's relief came down.

Next day at breakfast time in the mess room N remarked accusingly, "Jim where were you, I did not see you in the engine room last night when I came down?" By this time I had already enough confidence to challenge his doubtful expertise which was supposedly due to his seniority. My response was, "What time was it when YOU got down?" His response was "What is that got to do with it?" The second engineer had by now pricked up his ears and asked Leslie what is this all this about. He explained that my relief had already come down and he had told me to go topside and that it was some time later he could himself join me due to N's lateness. This implied that N was somewhat dilatory in assuming his duties. Suitably chastised by the second engineeer N was as sweet as pie for the rest of the voyage; unfortunately there is always one.

Nearing the UK homeward bound the chief engineer did the rounds to enquire who would be available for next voyage, I respectfully declined using the reason that I preferred to go back to Clan Line with the regular calls at Glasgow. In the event the enquiry was pointless as when stopped due to fog in the English Channel we heard that the ship, and her sister, had been sold to the Elder Dempster Line for their west Africa trade.

One trip was enough, and let's just say that during this voyage I realised the possible reasons for the difficulty they were having in recruiting engine room staff when one lad joined ship at London After taking an initial look at his cabin and a scan through the engine room entrance door he did an about turn and down the gangway he went with his suitcase still unopened.

At end of my voyage leave from this ship I was requested by Clan Line to join another Clan ship of similar vintage and machinery as the *Clan Urquart* but declined, and after sending applications to a number of shipping companies with steam ships was offered a position of fourth engineer with the venerable shipowners T.&J. Brocklebank.

Oddly enough I came across the chief engineer on the TSS *Umgeni* in surprising circumstances in Calcutta some years later. By then he was serving on a Clan Line ship. I was walking along the dockside on my way to my ship and happened to be passing that ship and lo and behold there was "'enry all from Uull" as we knew him, leaning rather disconsolately over the rail. I went aboard to greet him, and I learned the reason for his demeanour. Their chief steward had apparently not come across with sufficient bung to the local customs officer and as a result the ship's bonded store was closed, so I invited him to my ship and had a yarn and catch-up and a few beers, and I gave him a couple as a parting gift.

As I had only had initially three months' sea time, mostly spent on deck work overhauling cargo winches, and had never handled engine manoeuvring on my first ship I was a little surprised to be offered a berth as fourth engineer, especially as I knew I would be on watches by myself. My father's advice was to take it, anything I didn't know I would soon learn. In fact most of the engineering and deck officers were sailing in newly promoted positions, thus the average age was quite young.

This turned out to be a happy ship despite her age, having been built as far back as 1917 at Port Glasgow by Russell & Co and a was one of only two ships in the fleet that survived two wars. Although her sister ship had her bottom blown out and engine room wrecked by charges attached by Italian frogmen whilst moored at Gibraltar in May 1943, two years later she was refloated and towed back to the UK and repaired.

I joined the *Mahair* at Glasgow on the 23rd May, 1957, at the start of what was to be voyage number 94 after she had undergone a very protracted rebuild. This included four new boilers, main engine stripped and overhauled by the original makers, new pumps, accommodation refurbished, and something only her newest sisters in the fleet could boast, a proper sunken swimming pool abaft the funnel, not a wooden canvas lash up . Shipowners were even then still trying to

My painting of my first ship, SS *Maihar* (I), when joining T.& J. Brocklebank. Did two deeps sea trips between May 1957 and May 1958.

replace tonnage lost in the previous war, and refurbish others which had suffered from lack of maintenance due to the stress of war, and gradually rebuild their former trade routes.

After such a protracted lay-up in the hands of the ship repairers inevitably there were teething troubles. As an example, due possibly to a lack of familiarity with such relatively ancient engines, they fitted a cooling water pipe in a location that was severed when the cranks revolved, all of which came to light when we prepared to get under way, so much so that our final passage down the Clyde was marked by a number of stoppages. Given that us engineers had been working around the clock for the past few days it was decided to anchor off Ailsa Craig overnight to give us all a break before resuming sea watches.

The massive triple expansion reciprocating engine had cylinder diameters of 28ins, 48.5ins, and 84ins and a stroke of 54ins, possibly one of the largest units of its type afloat at that time. She had no remote temperature sensors; for example it was only by touching the crankshaft proper with fingers in the small gap between the bottom ends of the crankshaft and crank web as it revolved towards you that you could gauge if it was running hot. This practice was termed as, and was an apt description too, "feeling around", similarly with all the other moving parts, so a sense of smell and touch was the prime method of gauging the condition of the various moving parts.

We finally departed from the Clyde and sailed south around the UK to dock at Middlesbrough to start loading prior to our outward voyage. Middlesbrough was known to us serving with Brocklebank as the party town, and as a result was quite a favourite port. In these days before mobile phones the only connection with the outside world when in port was when a land line cable and connection was fitted on board.

Phone connection was then made by dialling the exchange and asking to put through to such and such a number, net result was on replacing the receiver it would then ring back with a call from the girls in the exchange asking when were we having a party on board. Our number soon got around and next would be nurses at the local hospital. The local Flying Angel mission was also a favourite haunt, with dances frequented by a bevy of attractive young ladies

Before leaving London at the start of the voyage the fifth engineer had bought two goldfish and if he happened to be on watch and it was rough weather it was common for anyone passing his cabin to look in and check if the bowl was secured safely. These survived as far as the Red Sea but when calling at Assab he had taken some sand from a beach there to put in the bowl. Obviously this did not agree with the fish as they both died shortly afterwards.

Our next loading port was Antwerp, and it was here that what could have unwanted repercussions occurred. With the chief officer and carpenter I paid a visit to a bar not far from our ship, and after leaving early in daylight next morning and making our way back to the ship the chief spotted some white wicker type chairs outside a, by now closed, café, whereupon he decided that one of these would be just the thing for the

In my cabin, wife-to-be photo on my desk!

bridge. Nothing daunted he purloined one and carried it up on his shoulder covered by his coat in a vain effort to conceal it. We had only gone about a hundred yards before a police car drew up. With such an appendage our companion was hardly inconspicuous, so naturally their curiosity was to be expected.

As the café and rest of the chairs were still in plain sight his explanation that he had bought it elsewhere cut no ice, so we were ordered to retrace our steps whereupon the officers roused the proprietor to ask if this was indeed one belonging to the café. The lady owner, opening an upstairs window, was either confused or surprised at being wakened at such an early hour by the law, or was being charitable bless her, stated that she could not be sure they belonged here. While

The aptly named Barren Rocks of Aden.

this discourse was taking place our hero whispered to us two, "let's make a run for it"! Oh aye, with two armed policemen, that'll be right. The smaller of the two officers was all for having us charged but the other, possibly seeing interminable paperwork looming just as the end of their shift approached told us to put the chair back and make tracks to our ship as fast as we could.

I got engaged to my girlfriend after my first trip with Brocklebank on SS *Maihar* and we got married at end of the next voyage. Aden was a favourite shopping stop, both from the bum boys alongside and ashore in the Crater, and for whatever reason I bought an electric iron to take home to give Ruby. As usually happens the girls in her office were always curious as to what I had brought home as a present, so you can imagine the banter from the girls when they finally managed to draw out the truth, their verdict being this guy is obviously serious. Actually electric irons were not in universal use in many homes – hot coals inside a steel iron being often still used.

Later when with friends I used to jokingly relate what happened when some time later I asked her father how they got on with the electric iron. "We did not like to say anything to you but I could not get it opened to put in the hot coals and I had to cut off a silly piece of wire hanging out the back". Cue Ruby to give me a dunt.

Our wedding photo, 11th June 1958.

CALCUTTA

Calcutta, now known as Kolkata, was our main unloading and loading port when outward bound was the longest port stay on the route it may be pertinent to recall some impressions of this fascinating city.

One of the most significant changes in world travel in recent years has been the availability and popularity of holiday destinations hitherto not considered as being either suitable or popular to merit promotion. Among these more unusual destinations, unusual that is to the casual holidaymaker, is the sub-continent of India, hitherto possibly considered as an outpost frequented by the backpacker determined to rough it and engage more closely with the native inhabitants, or as a more distant posting in the line of work.

Whilst the attractions of the India merit examination, and have a charm not found in many other locations, it has to be said that certain areas are not what one would normally choose as a holiday destination. With the exception of younger disenfranchised sons of well-connected families eager to make their fame and fortune, career civil servants, and those of the armed forces posted to India – who for long had laboured to stabilise the chaos prevailing in the vast nation amidst the myriad of factions and overlords, and brought some order and discipline, albeit based on British precepts of conduct – most of the impressions gained previously of the vast country were through the eyes of those serving in the Royal Navy and merchant navy.

On joining a shipping company which had a long-standing tradition of trading to India it was always at the back of one's mind that the arrival in India, to a first tripper at least, marked somehow a defining point in a rite of passage. Its various attractions, and also the more negative aspects, were long imprinted in one's mind on the outward voyage by the accounts related by more experienced shipmates. These were inevitably embellished in the telling, and truth to tell the anticipation was tempered with some trepidation as to what would be one's reaction.

As a taste of what was to come the arrival at our first port of call at Port Said gave one the first sniff of the mystic east, the air of odours, heat and dust assailed the senses and were wafted a long distance offshore, and could be savoured well before landfall. This was to be a foretaste of what was an entirely new world to a first tripper to the east.

The long-established shipping company T.&J. Brocklebank had been a major trader to the Red Sea ports and thence onwards to Ceylon, India and Pakistan with general and break bulk cargo, returning with gunny, cotton and other staple goods, a pattern of trade long vanished today. As an example, a seven month voyage I made in the late 1950s included almost 80% of the time in port, discharging, loading, or shifting ship, the actual steaming time on passage being the least proportion of the total voyage.

The port which contributed to the greatest delay and disruption to cargo discharge and loading was Calcutta, starting with an often long delay whilst waiting offshore at Sandheads for a pilot to take the ship up the tortuous river passage with its many shifting sandbanks to the port itself which was about 80 miles inland. On many occasions we joined up to a dozen or more ships lying at anchor at this exposed location, and during the monsoon season in July with its high winds we often had to steam around to dodge ships which were dragging anchors or had neglected to post a vigilant anchor watch. It was only later that I found out that Alan Halcrow from Hamnavoe had been the radio officer on the Nourse line's *Najarata* which had been moored a short distance away on one visit.

The pilot cutter was a fairly large handsome white-painted vessel, built by Lobnitz of Renfrew, and there was little warning when your turn came, a small powered open boat would be seen to approach the ship and this was the first indication it was our turn to travel up to Calcutta.

These pilot boats also performed a welcome duty in that when a Brocklebank ship was leaving the port they passed over incoming mail with the pilot on their outward passage which was then delivered on an ad hoc basis to any Brocklebank ships waiting at anchor whenever they felt inclined.

Typical scene in Kidderpore Dock at Calcutta.

Even when docked at Calcutta we seemed to be often at the whim of some distant authority. One day at this berth and another at a different one for no apparent reason. Shifting ship was inevitably done on Sunday, necessitating full sea watches and engine power, thus negating the chance of a day off, the fabled motto of the company was in port, "six days thou shalt labour, and on the seventh thou shall shift ship"! All of which meant that sea watches had to be manned for these duties.

The berth in the open Hooghly River some distance downriver from the massive steel structure of the Howrah Bridge was the most trying, especially in the monsoon season, the bore tides passed up and down twice a day which involved some very protracted mooring arrangements. Lengths of anchor cable had to be disconnected from the forward anchor chains and dragged aft to the stern from the forecastle, and ranged aft to be shackled to mooring buoys in the river to make sure the ship was securely anchored fore and aft.

Having long links with the port Brocklebank were wise to the problems and on most ships had fitted hawse pipe openings in each quarter to run the cables out to the buoys. However, this had not extended to the provision of additional chains aft for this purpose so long lengths had still to be unshackled and brought aft from the forecastle.

Depending on the strength of the tide surge the ship would rear up as much as six feet as if in the grip of some gigantic hand, the oncoming wave could be clearly seen approaching on the relative calm surface of the river, a sensation which was especially unnerving. I recall once seeing a small native craft being swept downriver along the side of the ship to become trapped under the foot of our gangway. Curiously even the birds sensed something was amiss, as there was usually a deathly calm preceding the passage of the wave.

The enclosed docks were reached from the river by locks and through a series of bridges. These were lifted or swung to let ships through, and during the time it took for a ship to pass through traffic would build up on each side of the waterway

At Calcutta swimming club. My pal Rankin Sinclair seated next to me was a fellow apprentice at Scotts' and was in port at same time on another ship in our company, lower is Ron McMurtrie 2nd Radio Officer on our ship.

waiting to cross, both on foot and on wheels of all descriptions, which can only be likened to a football crowd.

This scene was repeated each time any traverse took place during the twenty-four hours, both night and day; it is a city that literally never sleeps.

Calcutta was a fascinating place to the sailor, a total contrast of affluence and dire poverty. It was said that a third of the population were born, lived, and died on the pavement, and judging by the divergence between the levels of affluence and dire poverty this was no false claim.

As merchant navy officers we were somewhat privileged and had an entrée to various facilities perhaps not open to all. The excellent swimming club was an example of this, any white person from whatever country was welcome but no body of darker colour was welcome, even if it was their own country. All for 14 rupees for a fortnight, the equivalent of just over £1.

It was quite an experience to see an Indian "boy", often an elderly person with grown up family, running attendance on a young child in response to "Boy, come here and dry my feet", or "bring me a cold drink".

Chowringhee was the main street through Calcutta, and was bounded by many large buildings, including hotels and cinemas which, incidentally, had a no-smoking ban in force as far back as the mid-fifties. Many of the public buildings especially were large and impressive edifices, a relic of the British Raj, but some were showing signs of somewhat faded grandeur.

Off the main thoroughfares there was the inevitable warren of narrow back streets, the overall impression was one of a seemingly constant state of chaos and noise, with foot and vehicular traffic going in all directions, battered taxis, brightly coloured buses with passengers hanging on outside, horse- and peddler-pulled gharries, interspersed incongruously by spindle-shanked cattle wandering in and out of the melee.

Our usual mode of transport was using taxis, usually the locally assembled derivative of a Hillman Minx, comparatively cheap and not the relative extravagance in other countries. I well recall one occasion when three of us were being driven back to the ship late one evening; all was going well until the vehicle ran over a large hole in the road, with the engine then coming to a sudden stop. The driver went out and lifted the bonnet lid and tried all the usual remedies without success, after a while we went out to have a look, and it was then that we noticed that the engine mounts had broken off and the whole engine had dropped about six inches, with all the spark plug leads having been sheared clean off where they crossed a bracket.

Another memorable ride was when a few of us decided to travel in a horse-driven gharri, however we were one too many for the seating arrangements and the unfortunate radio officer ended up hung up by his elbows down between the shafts of the gharri with his feet just touching the road. Luck would have it that he had the shortest legs amongst us, and had great difficulty in keeping pace as he pattered along between the shafts to the great amusement of passers-by; his precarious situation was not helped by the fact that his face was right up against the stern of the horse!

As stated, the month of July was especially trying in the port, as being the height of the monsoon season when the humidity and temperature were especially high and the general climate was decidedly not conducive to heavy manual labour. Unfortunately this port of call was usually where the majority of the engine room maintenance was carried out, which on the *Maihar* consisted of unbolting, checking, and then re-assembling massive lumps of slippery and hot steel on the main engine, or contending with the savage heat radiated from the surface of the boilers when overhauling valves and other steam components.

Luckily our chief and second engineers had some compassion, and they amended our usual working pattern in port of 0800-1600 hours to the more bearable 0600-1400 to escape the worst of the heat, this also allowed a few hours ashore in the afternoon for all except the one engineer detailed as "day aboard" on the rota.

This ensured that there was always someone qualified to deal with any emergency aboard when sea watches were not set with the engine room fully manned. If he was lucky he would spend an otherwise peaceful 24 hours but if cargo was being worked then it was odds on that some emergency would occur either in the engine room or on deck with the cargo winches.

With three senior watchkeepers on board it was a boon to have your day aboard in port on Friday, as this ensured a couple of day's peace after work as day work stopped at 0100 hours on Saturday for the weekend unless moving ship or other such manoeuvres. Nevertheless one's off duty relaxation aboard was usually determined by the number of Brocklebank ships in port at the same time, it was not unusual to have several of the company's ships berthed simultaneously, and visiting former shipmates and making new acquaintances was the norm, all of which usually resulted in some merriment aboard or ashore.

It was homeward bound just shortly after we entered the Gulf of Oman whilst I was on the morning watch that I received a surprise call from the bridge that they were going to stop the ship, and just then the engine room telegraph rung a double ring for stop. On a steam ship this is not just a case of shutting the steam supply as various other systems had to be changed over etc. So after some frantic chasing round I got everything settled down and later went up on deck to see what was happening. Apparently when under way we had closed on a native sailing craft that had apparently made signals indicating that they had no fresh water aboard, so after we had come to a stop they came alongside and were passed down some canisters of water. As this is today a hot spot for piracy no ship now would ever take such action.

Homeward bound it was company policy to assess which officers wanted relieving for voyage leave immediately on arrival back in the UK and possibly preferring to rejoin after

We came across this native sailing craft when steaming
up the Gulf of Oman which had run out of fresh water.

leave, and those who were willing to stay with the ship around the coastal during unloading. A radio message to this effect was sent to the home office as we left Port Said homeward bound, normally 10 days for this ship, which gave the personnel department to make the necessary staffing arrangements.

This was my second voyage on the *Maihar* and Ruby was to make arrangements for our wedding at Greenock for early on our arrival back in the UK, but somehow the second radio officer got the dates wrong with result that my leave would be almost over before our marriage confirmation date. The company's engineering superintendent met the ship on arrival back in the UK, and on hearing my predicament and our wish to go to Jersey for our honeymoon and also up to Shetland for her to meet my folks, he gave me the welcome advice, "go home, get married, go for your honeymoon and let us know when you are ready to come back". This, I like to I think, epitomised the concern and attitude that the company took with their valued employees, amply borne out on a later occasion.

Jumping ahead a little, this was when after ticket leave and passing my second engineer exams I asked the company in November if I could have a short trip as my wife was expecting, due in February. They immediately assigned me to join SS *Matra* on the 15th November, 1960, for a relatively short trip on a Cunard charter, our parent company, as senior third engineer sailing from Liverpool to USA north and southern ports, back in early February. The trip was duly completed but our arrival back in London on 10th January coincided with the end of national service call up, which meant that there would be no call up for those abandoning a sea career.

Regrettably, many took this opportunity to leave without even waiting for their reliefs to arrive. I recall a Ben Line chief engineer officer coming aboard begging if we had anyone to spare for a harbour watch. Sadly we were similarly affected, and to make matters worse the ship was due to go up to Middlesbrough to undergo a protracted Lloyds Register survey.

Knowing of my long standing request to be relieved on arrival

I did three deep sea trips and two coastal voyages on my next ship, SS *Manipur* (III) between October 1958 and April 1960.

the company was in a dilemma in as much as they wanted someone who was familiar with the machinery to be present during this survey. I knew what was coming when I was asked to go to the captain's cabin, there to meet the engineering and marine superintendents. I was not, however, in my wildest dreams anticipating their suggestion. They offered to bring my pregnant wife down to Middlesbrough and put her up in a private ward for the confinement.

Grateful as I was for such an offer it reinforced my always positive impression of the Brocklebank company, but in saying that it is still pertinent to record that as in most companies what goes round usually comes round in the end.

After leaving the *Maihar* I spent a short time serving on a couple of vessels coasting around several ports in the UK and Europe, however it was my wish to go on deep sea voyages again, although many of my colleagues preferred to remain on coastal duties instead of extended foreign voyages. My next ship was the SS *Manipur* which I joined on the 29th October, 1958. She was one of the four sisters collectively known as the "black four," I assume because they were Brocklebank's first ships with water tube boilers and diesel generators, and generally thought of as workhorses. As borne out in my experience on the *Manipur*, they were prone to suffer from leaky boiler economiser tubes which necessitated repairs in confined, hot and asphyxiating conditions at the back of the boilers. They certainly were taxing but a side benefit was that promotion for engineer officers was remarkably swift as few wanted to do more than one trip. I did three trips on this ship, with the same chief engineer, and moved up a step each time! I signed off from her on the 25th April, 1960.

Just off watch, the SS *Manipur* was a hard worked ship and as such promotion came quick if you stuck it out.

As 3rd Engineer Officer on the *Manipur*, signs of a beard in this one.

SOME CHARACTERS
I SAILED WITH

Most merchant navy sailors will, I am sure, have come across many characters during their time at sea. I was fortunate to have been in the company of a number of those, who livened up and otherwise broke the monotony of a trip.

On the above ship our Scouse third engineer seemingly had a cargo stowage plan in his head or had tipped some dockers a few beers when loading, and knew where all the goodies were stowed, and subsequently during the sea voyage he could gain access to the cargo spaces without leaving any trace, being relied on to provide a supply of fruit juice, the best malt whisky, left shoes, heavy overcoats and umbrellas during the outward voyage.

On a voyage to the Indian continent via the Red Sea in the monsoon season the umbrellas, fruit juice and a dram could be useful and most welcome, but heavy raincoats and left shoes only were a little superfluous. The reason for left shoes only being shipped was ostensibly to discourage pilfering; the right shoe would follow on next ship!

He was also very adept at being able to avoid the nasty jobs in the engine room which were normally the third's responsibility. However he was a great source of exceedingly tall tales as well, a welcome quality to have on an often otherwise tedious voyage. He excelled himself on one trip. His otherwise happy marriage had not been blessed with any family, and his wife had unfortunately suffered a number of miscarriages. During this particular trip outward bound she was pregnant and he was hopeful of hearing some good news. Sadly the result was as before, and on hearing the unwelcome news during our stay at Calcutta the second engineer in deference to the third's upset frame of mind, granted him a respite from a turn-to for day work in the engine room on the day he had received the message.

Leaving India, through the Mediterranean and crossing the Atlantic to the States routine was as normal, and after calling at ports in the northern USA we then made our way down to the Mexican Gulf ports. It was here in New Orleans that one morning in port at the start of the day work routine that the second engineeer asked if I would carry out some task normally allotted to the third. After agreeing I then made the enquiry as to why he was not able to carry out his normal duties, my suspicions being immediately aroused as this was a particularly onerous task. His response was that the third had received the bad news from home that his wife had again miscarried and he felt that some leniency was appropriate in the circumstances.

"Hold on a minute, you are telling me she had a miscarriage twice in the same trip?" I asked. By then the second was rapidly retreating out the door of my cabin in the direction of the third's cabin, muttering "That lying b......, he nearly had me"!

Getting back to British India days, it was when in port on the *Manipur* some years later that on returning to the ship after a run ashore with some shipmates we chanced to pass the SS *Nyanza* in the same dock, a ship I had spent a period during my apprenticeship with Scotts', the builders, when she was under construction, "Come on," I said, "let's go aboard and see a real engine room". We duly trooped aboard and after I explained my interest we were kindly shown around the engine room by the helpful night duty engineer; in fact I was taking as much pride in the immaculate machinery as he was!

Passing through their engineers' accommodation on our way ashore we passed a cabin doorway of a good going party and were duly invited in, at the end of which we naturally extended our reciprocal invitation to our hosts to visit us next evening. Among the visiting party was a lad with a guitar and among his repertoire was a tune and song which to our surprise was in a foreign language. To our amazement our clearly very emotional Polish third engineer jumped up and with an obvious display of emotion embraced the singer and joined in with the complete words.

The explanation was that the singer was from Perthshire, and had lived near a camp for displaced Polish personnel during and after the Second World War and had picked up what was an apparently well-known Polish folk song, coincidentally native to the locality of our engineer Ted Wezdeki. His emotion was not surprising as he had been a child of the traumas of war and all the horrors of the Nazi invasion of Poland including losing trace of his parents who had probably been taken to a concentration camp. He had somehow survived to eventually make his way across Europe to finally end up in the UK.

The experiences had scarred him such that he always slept on his settee in his cabin and would not spread the carpet on the lino covered deck. In answer to my query for reasons he said that he had learned to be able to waken and jump immediately and not be hindered by climbing out of his bunk, and that there was a danger of the carpet slipping under his feet to hinder his getaway in an emergency, an ingrained fear from his horrific experiences in the past. There was not a day from then until we paid off that he did not embrace me and thank me for being responsible for that fortuitous meeting.

Many of the Brocklebank ships built after the end of the war had a Cochran fire-tube cylindrical donkey boiler to supply steam to the various auxiliary services when the main water tube steaming boilers were shut down in port. This boiler operated at only 100 psi, as all the winches and auxiliaries were electrically powered and received their current from diesel generators, so this boiler only served to give steam to water heaters and other minor items of machinery. Thus when all the major propelling machinery was shut down in port, with the engineers on day work, and off duty in the evening, native donkey men looked after this boiler on a twelve on, twelve off, routine.

However a rota ensured that one of the engineer officers had to take "night aboard", that is he had to be on board and on call, and sober, in case of emergency or other such duty. One of the unfortunate features of this boiler on the *Manipur* was that the oil fuel used to fire the burners had a habit of leaking out of the furnace nozzles if the orifices were not regularly cleaned and would drip down to spread along the fire bricks at the base. Given sufficient concentration this residue periodically went on fire, causing at times a fairly spectacular, if not dangerous, conflagration.

It so happened that one night in Calcutta, and given that they could be three or four of the company's ships in port at the same time the potential for beery reunions was distinctly probable, we were all in somebody's cabin savouring a few beers when the donkeyman came up from the engine room in a lather to say that there was a fire in the donkey boiler, and he wanted "burra sahib" to come down into the engine room, juldi.

The duty man on the night in question was the fifth engineer and his initial response was to tell him use one of the many portable canister fire extinguishers located around the engine and boiler room to put out the fire. It should be said here that in deference to his many other most admirable and personable qualities such as being a great raconteur, and guitar player, our fifth was not always first on the ball, as subsequent events will confirm.

In fact he never got over our displeasure in having to forgo any meaningful duties for most of the voyage due to his broken thumb and wrist, caused by having tried to start a lifeboat engine with his thumb around the handle, the inevitable result of a backfire was a broken digit.

In common with company practice our ship was equipped with numerous fire extinguisher canisters positioned strategically around the machinery spaces, plus a large capacity cylindrical canister mounted on a wheeled trolley for easy movement, and handily positioned on the starting platform near the donkey boiler, with a very long hose extension which could be used to reach in any major conflagration.

Notwithstanding the conviviality of the gathering in the cabin the fifths laudable dedication to duty finally overrode any annoyance at being disturbed, and he duly accompanied the donkeyman below to investigate. Half an hour later he reappeared, dishevelled, dirty and sweaty, with the comment that it was one hell of a fire, and had difficulty in reaching the source of the fire, such that he had to use every portable fire extinguisher in the engine room to quell the blaze.

In response to the common query of all us present that if the fire was so extensive why had he not used the large trolley wheel mounted extinguisher instead of setting off all the portable canisters, his response was "how do you expect me to carry that bloody great thing!

Part of the duty of the fourth engineer was to set off each week a different canister, re-charge with fresh chemicals, and attach a label with refill date and enter the relevant details into a log-book.

Our chief engineer on the SS *Maihar* was especially strict in enforcing this routine, as a former chief engineer in the company had been fired when, in response to a fire in the engine room, none of the extinguishers could operate and all were way past the refill date. As having earlier been a fourth engineer in the company on the above ship I could testify to the diligence in observing this routine to the satisfaction of the chief. There was no way was he going to be caught out in this manner. So we were all very conscious of his sensitivity to any fire, or equally important, any neglect of keeping refills up-to-date.

It was not unusual for two or three ships belonging to our owners to be in Calcutta at the same time and naturally when meeting up again with former shipmates this led to some marathon boozy sessions. On one such occasion one of the lads on a sister ship was prone to boast how he could out-drink anyone in the present company, so a competition was arranged based on the number of fairly large gin and tonics could be consumed by him and another lad. The procedure was that the same strength mixture would be poured into a pint glass each and the winner would be adjudged by the number consumed. He agreed to this and said when he came back from visiting the toilet he would take up the challenge. In his absence one glass had a meagre taste of gin added and topped up with tonic; the other had almost a full glass of gin and minimal tonic, the glass with the weak mixture being placed on the table in front of where he was previously sitting, the other strong one with his competitor.

Returning from his ablutions his first reaction was "I know all you crooked buggers you have given me a stronger mixture but I am not so daft, I am going to switch the glasses, so your trick did not fool me!" The inevitable result was that within minutes he was out for the count. I admit it was a silly trick to play but it was the inevitable result and representative of the work hard play hard culture then pertaining.

A longstanding friend of mine from our apprenticeship days in Greenock serving on another of our company's ship happened to be in Calcutta at the same time as ours so naturally we had a few nocturnal adventures. This particular meeting happened to be during the monsoon and to escape the worst of the heat and humidity our chief decreed that we work from 0600 to 1300 on port dayshift duties, a most welcome concession.

We were actually moored to buoys in the middle of Kidderpore Dock and on this particular night, due to the early start, I had turned in quite early and was not expecting my friend to come calling. Indications were that he was quite well lubricated when he resorted to banging on my, fortunately locked, cabin door exhorting me with such pleas as "I have come all the way to your ship, come on ashore ...".

Finally accepting my refusal with bad grace he then made his was down the gangway to the little sampan type craft lying alongside which provided means for us to get ashore to the dockside, and next I heard was the sound of empty bottles being thrown and smashed against the ship side below my cabin, he had obviously armed himself with a few which had been stored outside the galley. Our cabins were outboard against the ship's side with a wide internal alleyway, so I opened on of the portholes in my cabin and had some choice words to my pal as to his conduct.

The story does not end there, as next day the chief engineer called me to say that I was wanted by the captain, with no hint as to what was in store. I duly made my way up to God's country and first thing I noted was the extreme gloom as he had awnings rigged all round his accommodation and in complete contrast he had the artificial flickering flames in the mock fireplace lit.

His opening gambit was that the behaviour last night was completely unacceptable, a statement with which I concurred, and then I gave him a full explanation of the circumstances pertaining to the episode. He fully agreed that I was in no way complicit and with that I started to take my leave but was stopped in my tracks by his next comment, not quite believing what I had heard: "Hold on a minute, the worst part is that I get tuppence back on all these empty bottles!" In the dim light I could not ascertain if he was saying this in all seriousness.

You can well imagine the reaction when I reported back to our chief of the outcome of this meeting, he was torn between the thought that either I was spinning him a tale or the captain was having me on as he could not imagine him really being serious. Either way nothing more was heard of it.

When I think of characters I recall an episode on the SS *Matra* when we were at Panama City in Florida to load heavy rolls of paper. Our berth was apparently some distance from the town as I cannot remember ever having visited it. It had one of these very localised radio stations identified by a series of capital letters which we often tuned into in the evening, and on one occasion we heard the announcer saying that he had happened to drive past the dockside and had seen our ship and remarked on our Liverpool port of registry painted on the stern and went on to talk about the Beatles in this connection.

Our Scouse, but who else, electrical officer then called them up and told a fanciful tale of the Beatles such that they invited him up to the radio station for a more in-depth interview. By this time we were all tuned in and pretty well knew what was coming and he did not disappoint. "John Lennon, oh yes, he lived next door to us, biggest thief you ever met." "Paul McCartney? He used to go out with my sister until my father chucked him out of the house." "Ringo, he was my first cousin" ... and so on, you will have got the drift by now.

We often lay moored to buoys when in Kidderpore Dock in Calcutta and a couple of small Indian native sampan type craft would be laid on to take us back and forth to the shore, one would be stationed at the foot of our gangway and another at the shore, the boatman was usually a quite elderly man, often with some of his family bedding down aboard at night. He propelled the craft by a single oar at the stern standing slightly off to one side with what would be called a sculling action.

One evening returning to the dockside after a night ashore with some of my shipmates and embarking on the craft and noting that boatman was bedded down for the night I asked him to give me the oar, this request was greeted with some astonishment by both him and by my shipmates as you can well imagine!

Sculling and rowing small boats was second-nature to us boys during childhood in Hamnavoe, the difference being that we stood square on with legs apart for purchase and moved the oar sideways back and forth with a twisting action to impart the propulsive effect so it was no problem for me to propel our craft out to our ship. The result after this nocturnal demonstration was that in future every time any of the boatmen saw me approaching they proffered the oar all the while making a big show of lying at their ease! The story of the crazy Burra Sahib was soon spread in the boating fraternity.

Perhaps extended periods on ship abroad tended to

Indian boat.

encourage pranks and what otherwise can be termed childish harmless behaviour, I suppose being divorced from any contact with your otherwise natural environment and day to day contacts may encourage behaviour alien to what would be the accepted norm in everyday life ashore.

Perhaps illustrative of these seemingly childish actions was when some of us engineer officers bought small battery powered cars controlled by a long cable and small steering wheel from the bum boats at Aden. This was however not the whole story, as they then chalked-marked numbered "parking spaces" on the deck outside the ship's dining saloon, "driving" their own car along the deck and parking in their designated space.

A previously well-rehearsed routine would include a "driver" bursting into the saloon at meal-times complaining vociferously that someone else had parked in "his" reserved parking place! Cue fake arguments and much banter, "too bad, you should have come earlier" and so on. Such pranks caused the captain to whisper an aside to our chief at their table: "Chief are you SURE your guys are OK?"

Another harmless prank was when we all grew substantial beards and homeward bound all of us shaved off one side only, then march in to the saloon together with heads turned such that the hirsute side was plain to see, then in unison a smart turn to port to show the shaven side. By now the captain thought he had seen it all.

A prank that had no upside for me whatsoever occurred when we were moored in Colombo harbour. Together with the fifth engineer I was carrying out some maintenance on one of the cargo winches right up forward on the main deck and when completed I gently kicked a small empty cardboard box towards the ship's rail. He and I often had fairly robust but friendly exchanges on the merits or otherwise of football, me, versus rugby, him, and I should have suspected something when he challenged me to kick the empty box out over the top of the bulwark and over the side.

No problem says I, running full tilt down the steep sheer of the foredeck and gave it my best, to say I got a shock was an understatement, he had positioned the empty box over the top of a large eye plate welded to the deck! My shoe burst completely open and the pain in my toe was excruciating, so much so that I had to go ashore and have it X-rayed in a hospital, verdict was two broken toes. Our second engineer had a dilemma, as to who was most to blame, the fifth for playing a silly prank or me for falling for it!

A postscript to the tale was when coming back to the ship from hospital in the agents' launch our captain, who happened to be onboard, in his apparent concern for me, when looking over his shoulder missed the bottom platform of the overside gangway and put one foot in the water!.

To those of us calling at Vizakhapatan in the 1960s the cargo handling facilities seemed rather primitive, especially loading iron ore. The method employed was to rig a series of bamboo stages up the ship's side from the quay, and squad of females, mostly girls, would pass up a basket full of ore to the next stage where it would then be passed up again and so on until reaching the deck, where the basket would be then tipped into the hold.

It was no coincidence that at the end of their working day our inboard rail was fairly well crowded with onlookers, looking forward to our treat to observe them having an impromptu shower under a convenient water hydrant on the dockside, albeit still clad in a sari or similar enveloping garment although when fully wet it did nothing to hide their shape! Our offer of a fragrant soap, such as the ubiquitous red bars of Lifebuoy Toilet, could sometimes induce a more revealing display, however plain carbolic soap bars merited no such reward.

Our chief steward however went one better by persuading one of the most comely girls to come aboard with the inducement of a colourful sari, scented soaps and lotions and some other enhancements, and stood guard whilst she showered and finally reappeared looking absolutely gorgeous!

The two electricians on the *Manipur* worked a day-work pattern with Saturday half-day and Sunday off. Normally when at sea boat and fire drill took place on Saturday afternoon, but the second electrician, Harry, was very loath to give up his Saturday afternoon siesta after a few beers at lunch time for the so called Board Of Trade sports. "Why should he get away with it?" was the precursor of a trick to get his attention on one occasion.

During boat drill one of the lads donned a lifejacket and oilskins and rang the abandon ship bell outside his cabin and threw open the door, shouting "abandon ship! Abandon ship!" while another lad threw a bucket of water in through his open porthole directly above the settee where our reluctant hero was dozing. That certainly got his attention. He was a good shipmate and took it all in good part.

The next trick gave him even more palpitations; this was when he was removing for overhaul a fairly heavy fan motor which was fitted at about waist height in one of the engine room vent trunking up on the boat deck. Prior to him starting this task he came down to the engine room to warn the watchkeepers not to stand below the vent trunk whilst he was working just in case anything dropped, a timely warning and much needed as in the tropics under this vent gave a welcome blast of cooler air.

I am not sure what happened but lo and behold did he not drop the fan motor which fell down the vent trunk and crashed down on to the platform in the engine room. Quick as a flash one of the watchkeepers lay prone on the platform under the open vent and we covered him with a length of canvas. You can well image the fright the electrician got when he hurried down the engine room ladder to retrieve the motor and firstly saw the other watchkeeper leaning on the desk apparently sobbing and then to crown it saw two feet sticking out under the cover and the fan motor nearby!

He was the cause of his own misfortune once when he was replacing one of the heavy electric winch motors. It was suspended from a chain-block hoist under the control of one of the Indian helpers whilst Harry had his fingers on top of the mating base unit to ensure the thin metal shims were located properly when the motor was lowered on the securing studs. On receiving the signal to lower the helper quite properly lowered the motor but in doing so trapped Harry's fingers, "arria" he screamed, "juldi arria", (quickly lower) a command on which naturally the motor was lowered even further and by this time the full weight was on his digits. His command of the Hindustani "Bat" (language) never being his good point

My last trip in MN was on SS *Matra* (III).

– he should have said "avis" which means hoist, the opposite of "arria!" Luckily the helper's command of English was better than Stan's of Hindustani, and in the end the problem was solved by his despairing command, "just lift the bloody thing up".

My last deep sea voyage in the merchant navy was on the SS *Matra* leaving Liverpool on 24th November, 1960, and returning to London on 9th January, 1961, a relatively short trip to New York and a few southern USA ports. We experienced a near hurricane all the way out across the Atlantic as soon as we cleared Northern Ireland and as we were more or less light ship with a large number of crates containing boxes of bottled malt whisky and about a dozen Rolls Royce Silver Wraith limousines and a very small amount of general cargo it was a very uncomfortable journey.

As we were on a charter voyage from Cunard we docked right in the middle of New York, in what was in fact the Queens' berth, so a five-minute walk took us right on Broadway. As I recall it was the coldest I have ever experienced anywhere, all the external piping on the ship froze up and even a deep breath was painful. When the hatch covers were removed the result of our gyrations across was evident when it revealed some of the heavier pieces of cargo which had been stowed in the tween decks wings had fallen on top of some of the limousines resulting in damage.

During the voyage the carpenter, who dipped the double bottom tanks daily, enquired of the engineers a number of times on our way across the Atlantic if we had been repeatedly transferring water to the fore peak tank as no matter how much he took out it was always full. The reason for his query was revealed when we went into drydock at Middlesborough and we found that part of the shell plating right down forward had sprung and some of the rivets had sheared, hence the leakage. For this to happen on such a solidly constructed vessel demonstrated the pounding we had experienced on the way across.

Close attention was given to the whisky storage in the tween decks by an unnamed engineer when loading, with the result that some of the contents must have suffered considerable evaporation by the time it came to unload (this was always the explanation given by the puffermen when freighting the nectar from the distilleries to Glasgow!). Be that as may the engineers' bar bill was minimal, so much so that the chief steward remarked to our chief engineer that he must have been pleased to have such an abstemious bunch of lads, all they seemed to sign for was mixers and the odd beer. As the chief was in on the secret he could just but nod knowingly. The It'll Do Bar was a favourite watering hole for Brocklebank ships when in New Orleans; practice was to bring the manager a bottle of Scotland's best, and one for ourselves, place it on the table cowboy film style, and just order mixers and enjoy the ambience.

As noted earlier what was to be my last trip coincided

with, but was not related to, the end of national service. I respectfully declined the company's offer of moving my then pregnant wife to Middlesbrough but was allowed to go home for a weekend to check all was well. By that time it was suspected that twins were in the offing. Unfortunately I developed a severe chill travelling home from London and was signed off for sick leave and to my regret was not able to rejoin the *Matra*.

All was well at home and on return was posted to other ships in UK ports. It was whilst serving on SS *Mangla* that I received the unwelcome news that twin boys had been delivered but sadly the first was stillborn. I was allowed to go back home immediately and it was then, after discussing with my wife who naturally was in some distress, that I decided to make the break and look for shore employment. This decision was in part due to the realisation that at that stage of my life it was either that or study for remaining certificates of competency and make a career at sea, I also felt that my wife could do with some additional support in light of our recent misfortune.

LOOKING BACK

There were many memories of life on board ship that one can truly cherish. To come off watch when in the middle of the ocean and lean on the rail on a moonlight night and trace the ship's wake on the surface of a calm sea comforted by the whine of the turbines or whump, whump of the triple expansion engine down below was something to be savoured.

One of the most satisfying aspects of seagoing was when operating the engine controls when manoeuvring on entering or leaving port and knowing that you were responsible in answering the engine room telegraph orders for the safe movements of the ship. A feeling that was multiplied many times at the end of a voyage when you stepped on to the quay and thought back on all the usual travails, long engine room watches in very hot conditions, breakdowns, the usual disagreements and so on, and to see your ship safely tied up after bringing home a full cargo through storms, calms, and everything that the ocean could throw at you; and knowing that you had played your part.

Another cherished memory was the companionship and solidarity with your shipmates which fortunately was the rule rather than the exception – most disagreements were settled with a couple of beers off-watch. Many, whose apparent foibles and idiosyncrasies viewed at close quarters onboard would possibly be considered odd ashore, added to the variety and humour in the tedium of a long voyage. Overall it is my firm opinion that the at-times much maligned Scousers were the best shipmates!

(Note the dates given for joining and leaving ships are dates of signing articles as shown in my discharge book, the actual dates of joining and leaving might vary.)

LIFE ASHORE

Following the birth of my son, Brocklebank arranged for me to stand-by a ship in drydock at Glasgow which allowed me to travel home most nights. But in the end I made the decision to resign and seek employment ashore. It was decision time; make a career at sea or look to progress in a chosen field that could utilise my experiences to date.

My first job ashore was as a tool setter with an American company in Port Glasgow who manufactured clip-on terminals for electric cables of all sizes, no criticism of the company but the change of environment was somewhat traumatic and unsettling, and after a short time I looked for something different. Always having been interested in draughtsmanship I applied for a vacancy in the steam turbine drawing office advertised by AEI of Trafford Park Manchester, and following interview was offered the job, this was in May 1961. This was something of a test as I had never actually worked in a drawing office previously, but sea experience with turbines and something of an aptitude for technical drawing stood me in some stead.

I initially lived for about six months in lodgings in the suburb of Chorlton-Cum-Hardy outside Manchester, I suppose reckoned to be a fairly up market area. I learned later Sir Matt Busby, when manager of the Manchester United football team had once lived there. I shared a room with two students, a sixpence coin was needed for both the water heater and the TV in the communal room and we were allowed a bath once a week.

This period coincided with cricket test matches and two of the residents, a Jamaican and an Indian, were naturally keen followers of the games which could be seen on a sixpence coin-slot TV in the common room. Out of interest I used to accompany them, but one evening the landlord came to complain that the noise was too loud, which we doubted as we were well away from his quarters – sadly it was just his perverse nature. So for succeeding evenings for a prank we all decided to just sit talking among ourselves with no TV on. We did not have long to wait before the landlord came to ask, "No TV on?" We knew the reason for his interjection; no TV meant he was getting no sixpences!

However, in November 1961 I was able to buy a three-bedroom semi in Urmston, a nice suburb south of Manchester with easy access to Trafford Park. This was quite a change for my wife, bringing her to a strange area in middle of winter with a nine-month-old baby, who at that stage was not able to walk, and I still admire her resourcefulness in setting up home and finding her way around shops and the new surroundings, something she was to repeat in other moves in the UK and abroad.

The work in the drawing office was interesting, especially when we were designing the steam turbine machinery for two Royal Fleet Auxiliary ships, one, the RFA *Regent*, being built by Harland & Wolff at Belfast and the other the RFA *Resource*, by Scotts' at Greenock, my old alma mater. Nearing the completion of the designs and finalising of the machinery arrangement the chief draughtsman asked me to go up to Scotts' to discuss some details, and it was a somewhat novel experience to fly up to Glasgow and then be picked up and driven down to Scotts' at Greenock in a chauffeur driven Austin Princess car! Some change from my apprentice days.

I enjoyed my time with my colleagues at AEI but hankering back to Greenock I subsequently was interviewed and offered a similar drawing office position in Scotts' engine drawing office. Ruby was naturally pleased to be back with her family and friends again. It was whilst working here that I learned of my mother's passing. I knew she was terminally ill from a recent visit I had made when she was in hospital but the pain was no less, especially as she was only 56 years old.

I got leave to travel up to Shetland for the funeral. At that time the flight north left from Renfrew Airport at Abbotsinch but unfortunately on that day they were cancelled due to fog in Shetland – nothing unusual there – so I was not able to attend the funeral. When I reported back to the drawing office later that day the chief draughtsman enquired as to the reason for my return and, on hearing the reason, he kindly told me to take a few days off so I could make other travel arrangements.

I was, however, able to attend the funeral of my late father, who had lost his life in a boating accident whilst working at his lobster creels in our small boat at the South Voe of Papa in fairly bad weather in October. Somewhat ironic, as he been a fisherman all his life and had served for most of the Second World War in the Royal Navy in various hazardous theatres of the conflict.

After a few years with Scotts' I began to look for something more allied to original design as compared to just draughting. Sadly Scotts' was later to fall foul of the various machinations of various government agencies tasked with the survival of what was left of the British shipbuilding industry, an industry which had many detractors. Leaving Scotts' I was able to move to a project design office with Joy Sullivan, an American company in Greenock who manufactured coal mining machinery and air compressors. I was in a small team engaged on design of some new prototype machinery and looking at improving the design of existing machinery. This resulted in me being involved in some preliminary trials in the works and later for a period having to travel weekly to a coal board proving ground in England to set up and test run and subsequently re-design and modify some items on a type of underground stone wall packing machine. Unfortunately in the end the concept was faulty for the intended purpose and was abandoned.

Having got a taste of project work of this kind, and feeling that my efforts and contribution out in the field so to speak, outwith the actual drawing office, was being undervalued I got the oft repeated, but too late, story. When handing in your notice your boss would say "but we were going to give to a rise in recognition of your efforts". I then moved to a local company in either 1973 or 1974 which was part of the large multinational John Swire group. Here I was initially responsible for preparing quotations and design of a variety of marine equipment for ships, mainly oil tanker tank hatches fitted with a fairly unique and very popular and efficient hatch lid opening gear. These items were very popular and well regarded in the industry, and in addition to sales to UK shipyards a large order book was ensured by our European agents.

The Swire company had just built a new factory at Inchgreen, Greenock, after adding a well-known local company which specialised in pipework for a wide range of industrial applications to its existing small factory. The formal opening was to be carried out by John Swire, or Jock as he was well known. In preparation to this event a new flagpole had been made and erected in the grounds fronting the new building. Unfortunately, in the rush to have everything ready, much of the paint had been scuffed off when it was positioned and yours truly had the job of touching up the damage. This involved in rigging a bosuns' chair which then hoisted me to the top of the – considerable – height to apply new paint.

I also had to hoist the Swire houseflag which I had already folded so that a tug on the halyard by Mr John Swire would fully open it when he declared the facility open; cue much clapping by all the assembled staff, agents and local dignitaries etc. etc.. Naturally I had rehearsed this procedure many times to avoid the indignity of a false start. Fortunately all went to plan and, after the unfurling, Mr Swire handed the halyard back to me to make fast.

Being a relatively new employee it said much for the Swire's that Mr John Swire, chairman of the large multi-national group and great grandson of the founder John Swire (1793-1847), sought me out afterwards at the formal function to thank me for a job well done.

Opening of the new John Swire factory at Greenock by the chairman John Swire, I was taking the halyard to belay on the flag pole.

My responsibilities were soon enlarged also to be in charge of the whole fabrication and machining departments, a process that proved to be a whole new learning curve, with the shop floor staff reporting directly to me through the foremen. In a unionised establishment this often led to some interesting, heated, and enlightening moments. But overall I could not complain of not having full cooperation in implementing a number of design, production and working improvements. I think the overriding advantage was a generally perceived impression that you knew what you were talking about and was not trying to bluff the work force.

A somewhat amusing aspect of the earlier mentioned situation regarding the religious divide in the west of Scotland used to occur when recruiting welders or platers for the fabrication shop. I would duly interview a candidate and if suitable would offer him a job, his religion being immaterial in my eyes. Guaranteed within a few days of him starting Pat, one of the boilermakers union reps. in the fabrication shop, would come knocking on my door: "Can I see you for a minute Jim?" "Sure, come in, what is it Pat?" "This place is getting like Masonic Lodge" he claimed.

Mindful that this particular department shop worked on a pool bonus system the resultant value of which depended on all pulling their weight I asked "Is he a good worker pulling his weight and getting on with his colleagues?" "Oh yes, no problem" "he replied. "That's all I need to know then, I am not concerned as to what his religion is."

The same performance would occur if a new hire happened to be Catholic. This time it would be Andy at my door: "Jim, this place is getting like Chapel" and the same dialogue would ensue and he would go away satisfied. I must emphasise that I personally never experienced any difficulties in the running the department due to different religions; I think it was evident to the workforce that I treated everybody the same, the only thing that counted to me was their skills.

It also fell to me to make many visits to shipyards in the

UK and abroad, either to discuss customers' requirements, or less happily to attend to some actual or perceived complaint. I recall one visit especially to a small shipyard at Busum in northern Germany where we had supplied some complete circular hatch covers with long coamings which extended down through a second deck on a chemical tanker. The complaint was that the circular openings on the hatches already fitted were out of circularity and the lids did not seat properly.

This baffled me, as we religiously subjected all lids and hatch coaming tops to a chalk test to check sealing and alignment etc. It was when I was checking the identical hatches we had made stored in storage at the shipyard intended for the second ship of the series, and noting all was well, that I realised that some misalignment and distortion must have been caused when they welded the coamings to the two decks. I reported this to the manager involved, who grudgingly agreed with my reasoning, and with some obviously blasphemous and derogatory comments addressed to some of his underlings – which needed no translation – indicated I was then free to go.

I took the train back to Hamburg and from my hotel called our German agent with the good news, he had been waiting with some trepidation as obviously had the reported fault been due to us it would not helped his reputation for any future orders. He called back to base in Greenock with the result and ordered a bottle of champagne!

I had visited him on many occasions for meetings with German shipbuilders. We often felt, perhaps not always justifiably, that he was loath to back us sufficiently vigorously in any dispute re quality, delivery etc and tended to favour the customer, the shipbuilders. Since he had other irons in the fire, and was also agent for other marine products, he was obviously not wanting to queer his pitch with potential customers. He usually booked me in a hotel near his house in Hamburg and we would often continue our meetings in his office upstairs, some of which got a little heated, but back downstairs he was the absolute perfect host and all acrimony was forgotten.

With me on a trip to a shipyard at Kiel to instal some fittings on a tanker I had a welder from our works to assist, plus a representative from an outside supplier. One evening we decided to visit the town centre and noted what seemed to be a fairly respectable night club with good music, and so duly made our entrance and got seated to enjoy the ambience and some drinks.

The establishment had what was obviously the resident crooner but later on in the night, and after some lubrication, to our surprise and concern, my accomplice called over one of the waiters and announced that he wanted to get up and sing. By this time the rest of us were trying our best to be invisible and not betray any sign of being in his company. To our, and all the rest of the audience, great surprise he was a wonderful singer, bringing the house down with his initial rendering of San Francisco! So much so that due to popular demand he had to do quite a few encores, naturally we were now basking in his reflected glory and enjoying free drinks. By then it was noticeable that the resident vocalist was getting a bit peeved that his thunder had been well and truly stolen, so to great acclaim our lad duly and somewhat reluctantly made his departure from the stage.

We had agents in Germany, Holland, Denmark and Norway, although I had most contact with the German and Dutch agents. I became very friendly with our Dutch agent, Cees Tettelaar who had been an excellent footballer as a youngster during the time of the German occupation of Holland and, whilst foodstuffs became increasingly scarce, his prowess and popularity in his local area resulted in the butchers and grocers there managing to supplant his family's meagre rations to allow him to keep up his performance.

This all ended, however, when his parents were visited by the local SS to demand information as to his whereabouts as he was at an age that would render him liable for transportation to works camps or worse. They fobbed them off for a while until they were given the option of surrendering him or themselves being deported, a dilemma with resulted in his incarceration.

I am not sure where he was interred but he said there were many eastern Europeans including some with obvious mental deficiencies who were as a rule maltreated and reduced to starvation. He said that it took him a long time afterwards to sleep properly as he had to be alert at all times as some of these poor wretches would think nothing about cutting off a fleshy portion of a leg of anyone unwary in an effort to assuage their hunger.

These circumstances has resonance with the precautions noted earlier affecting Ted Wyzdecki.

Cees had bought the same model, number and colour of an Alfa Romeo car each time he changed vehicles, his theory was that when visiting a shipyard looking for business, this, with his habit of donning an old cap, would impress the observers with his frugality and real need to obtain an order, Poor Cees, he is really struggling, same old banger, do we have anything we can throw his way!

A more interesting trip, if I can call it that, was when I spent a couple of months at the large Hyundai shipyard in South Korea to fit a special type of stern gland we had manufactured destined for of a series of cargo ships built for Kuwait Shipping Co. I had not been involved in the design of this product which had been developed by an outside agency, but the person who was normally responsible, for an albeit simpler design, was deemed to be unsuitable for such a task, possibly as earlier he had been intending to travel to Belfast to meet a customer but got off at the Isle Of Man instead and wondered why they did not all speak like the Rev. Ian Paisley!

To be honest I had doubts about this design and felt it was too complicated for such an arduous duty. The principle, without being too technical, basically embodied three split-rings, one bolted to the rotating propeller and the other fixed

Hyundai shipyard, with a super tanker and cargo ship building in same dock, note staging on the smaller ship.

to the outside of the stern tube, with a central rotating ring which was held against and rubbed against the hull fixed ring to make the seal due to the pressure of a split rubber ring. The two halves of the rubber ring were joined by means of a heated and chemically coated vulcanising unit all within the narrow confines of the assembly, the selling point being that it was possible to dismantle the whole assembly without removing the propeller.

This shipyard was a real eye opener, spread over a vast area with huge building docks and straddle travelling cranes and up-to-date steel fabrication machinery, and a tremendous work ethic. Somewhat ironically, prior to construction of the shipyard a number of their technical staff had spent a period in the Lithgow shipyard at Port Glasgow, who supplied designs of the first two tankers Hyundai built, ostensibly to "Learn them how to build boats!" They certainly learned how to build boats alright, and learned only too well, the evidence is there for all to see now.

My flight took me first to Tokyo and then my flight to Seoul in South Korea was from Osaka. Here I had a bizarre experience. Whilst at the entrance to the airport two cars came to a screaming halt outside and a man with blood running down his face shot out of the first vehicle and dashed towards the door while another from the second was waving what looked like a weapon in his direction. I was either foolhardy or brave but I managed to shoot off a photograph. The reason for all this commotion was that they were apparently filming a Japanese version of James Bond! The flight touched down at Alaska en-route to South Korea and it was a little disconcerting during this flight to look out the window and see the ruins of a crashed plane lying on the mountains far below.

As it was impossible to obtain the Korean currency Won outside Korea I had to take a substantial amount of American Express Cheques. This posed a problem when I boarded a taxi outside Pusan airport, not helped by the driver's complete lack of English. First problem was to explain where I wanted to go, saying Hyundai meant nothing as there were numerous facilities under that name. In the end I drew a small sketch of ships and cranes which seemed to do the trick.

We seemed to drive for ever, well outside any conurbations and into the countryside, and realising that I still had no local currency managed to explain to the driver that I needed to go to a bank. Luck would have it when we did find a bank it was closed for the day so there was nothing for it but to go direct to the shipyard. On arrival, after introducing myself to my contact he ushered me up to his office and said he would go back and arrange payment.

Much to my surprise when he came back he was sporting a most noticeable bloody cut on his lip. In answer to my query he said, "bloody taxi, they are all crooks, he said he had taken you on a long detour to find a bank, but was just a trick to try and get more money!" They apparently had fisticuffs as a result. In the circumstances I thought it was better I did not confirm that the taxi driver had indeed made a long detour.

Given the and up and down nod of the head indicated "no", and a shake of the head meant the opposite, you can well imagine the problems I had with the Korean shipyard workers in assembling and testing the stern glands.

On my return I was very surprised to note the scepticism voiced by some Lithgow staff as to the likely future prospects for the Hyundai shipyard – comments such as "they canna build boats on a bowl of rice a day". Little did they know their own future was already in peril. This was somewhat ironic as a number of Hyundai staff had spent a period at Lithgow's in Port Glasgow, as noted above, learning how to build ships, they were obviously quick learners!

In saying that they had the advantage of a clean slate and could lay out the shipyard on what could be termed a green field site, unhampered by any established roads and houses, and took full advantage of this to establish a state of the art facility equipped with modern fabrication, and later, machining capacity to allow the construction of large diesel engines.

My impression was that the labour force was diligent and hard-working, with an obvious desire to show the rest of the world what they could do. At that time such items as steering gear, main engines and cranes were all being supplied by European companies, possibly the long-standing enmity to Japan precluded any equipment from that source, and naturally these suppliers were providing personnel to oversee installation and commissioning of their products.

So we were a disparate bunch, housed in the aptly named Foreigners Hotel, quite basic but adequate accommodation, and we ate in a communal dining room. Whilst I will never submit to anyone in my admiration of the Hyundai shipyard staff in what they had achieved, I have to say, and am not alone in this opinion, that the food served was definitely not cordon bleu!

Not what we expected; good honest grub would be fine, but let's just say our tastes differ. With the outside temperature gradually hotting up we managed to implore the canteen overseer to provide the ingredients which could be served as a salad, such as cold chicken, lettuce etc. With great anticipation we trooped in one evening ready to enjoy what we would call a proper meal, to be confronted with several bowls filled to the brim with what looked like mayonnaise. "Where is the salad?" we enquired. "In there" was the reply. His explanation was that somehow or somewhere he had seen diners spreading salad cream on their salad, so decided to make a proper job of it and fill the bowl!

As I said, this shipyard was built on wholly undeveloped land, and a whole small township had sprung up to serve it, among which was a barber shop, staffed by very attractive girls. It so happened that the representative from Harland & Wolff overseeing the installation of their engines in a series of ships for Kuwait Shipping Company had very blond hair, something which these girls had apparently never seen before, this novelty was such that they almost fought one another to have the privilege of cutting his hair! Such was the remote locality that many inhabitants there had never seen a Caucasian in the flesh, the small schoolchildren in particular would just stop and stare in wonderment.

It was obvious that Hyundai, and its many tentacles in a multitude of industries, had much sway with the South Korean authorities. This was evidenced forcibly when the USA representative of the manufacturers of the steam turbines for several tankers decided that he had carried out his duties and fully commissioned the machinery to an accepted standard, albeit being disputed by Hyundai, presented himself with ticket and passport at the boarding gate at Pusan airport en-route back to USA. "Oh no," said the guard, "Hyundai say no" so nothing for it but return to the shipyard. They were very touchy about letting us representatives go. A short time earlier during a shipping slump some Greek owners did a midnight flit by hiring a small boat to make the clandestine short sea passage across to Japan leaving the shipyard with two almost complete tankers.

I have to admit to some trepidation when I took my leave

from Pusan, my passport photo was scrutinised intently and from photo to my visage several times before I got the nod. A final note to this interesting episode was that on arrival at Tokyo airport, en-route to London, while stuck in interminable queues to complete some complex form, I heard my name being called on a Tannoy to go to a certain desk. To say that I was surprised to hear the name Pottinger in Tokyo airport is an understatement, but to my everlasting gratitude I was hustled through seemingly endless corridors and even kitchens to a waiting van, with luggage, to take me direct to the plane. Apparently BA had decided that given the delays in processing all the relevant documents I would never catch my flight. So hats off to them.

It was a happy time working for Swire but all this later became overshadowed by the contraction and consolidation in the shipbuilding industry, and finally nationalisation. Seeing what was in the wind I decided that it was time to make a move before the full impact became a reality, and opportunities due to the expansion in the oil industry beckoned.

Incredible as it seems now our sales manager had been sent to Aberdeen in the early 1970s to assess if there was any potential market for our products which included general fabrication and a long standing industrial pipework division. His verdict on return was, "It's all a flash in the pan." This reminds me of the old adage that when a salesman travels to a supplier and obtains an order it is a sales trip, if unsuccessful then it was a marketing trip!

I duly applied for a manufacturing superintendent position in Vetco Offshore, a USA owned company in Aberdeen, initially interviewed at the Glasgow offices of what was then the labour exchange, another in their offices in Aberdeen, and then finally by the company which I subsequently joined in October 1977. With the oil industry expanding at such a high rate – this was in 1977 – it was only by recruiting outside Aberdeen that all vacancies could be filled. Thus part of the

Marina houses from flight between Los Angeles and Oxnard California.

Muckle Loch where most of us learned to swim, a bit nippy
when the sea washed in over the outer edge at high tide.

conditions included a full removal and resettlement package and they duly put me up for nearly eight months in a local hotel before selling our house in Greenock and buying another in Aberdeen.

Whilst the company was meeting costs of lodging, breakfast and evening meal in the hotel it still behoved one not to try and take advantage by inflating one's expenses claim. Another employee on the same arrangement had the temerity to add the cost of post-dinner brandies and cigars to his expenses, a bounty that was soon to end when the personnel manager enquired if that was the normal nightly practice at home.

As you can imagine, working in an American owned company we naturally picked up some of the characteristics of their homeland. Among many of the positives was modern machine tools, but as time went on and we gained confidence in design and manufacturing methods and procedures in a wholly new environment, it became evident that we were often the dog with our friends in California and Houston wagging the tail!

Highlights were several trips to the main plant in Ventura on the Pacific Coast of California about 100 miles north of Los Angeles, with a sublime climate to enjoy. It was with some envy when visiting some of the staff's homes we noted nearly all the near residents had their own boats tied up to a berth adjoining their house.

I recall once swimming in the hotel's outside pool during what would be their winter and as such was the subject of some curiosity as it was unheard of to be in the unheated water at that time; to me it was a lot better than the Muckle Loch at Hamnavoe! The flight from the UK landed at Los Angeles and it was a short hop from there to Oxnard followed by a short taxi ride from Ventura. This flight was with a very small plane, which in fact was parked more or less under the wings of a jumbo jet, and after boarding through a rear door the pilot used the same entrance, and after seating in the cockpit called out "would the nice lady sitting next to the door give it a good bang to ensure that you have shut it properly". What could certainly be called a novel flight instruction!

At that time the industry was booming, and on-time delivery was most important, so priorities took precedent with the usual pattern of two shifts and weekend working in the manufacturing departments.

One of our products was drilling risers manufactured from heavy thick wall tubing with substantial connectors at each end. In this instance the risers were destined for a dynamically positioned drill-ship and connected to the wellhead. The connectors had been welded to the casing by a sister company but unfortunately inspection showed considerable faults in these welds, and I was tasked with going out to southern Spain to organise repairs to the connectors which were stored on the harbour side at Puerto De Santa Maria, the bay just across from Cadiz.

To help with the language a colleague from our office in London was to accompany me initially as he had spent some time living in Spain and could speak the language reasonably well. We took the flight from London to Jerez, I cannot remember which airline it was but am pretty sure it was a small outfit as when I tried to pay for a drink with Scottish banknotes the stewardess said it did not have parity with an English note, however an Irish note did! You can imagine my reaction to that, and much merriment by my English colleague.

We were put up in quite a comfortable hotel, the Caballo Blanco, the white horse, not too far from the harbour and after hiring a car basically went round the local watering holes to ask if anyone knew of any likely contacts able to carry out the weld repairs. We did anticipate some luck as there was a large offshore steel fabrication company some miles further up the coast so were pretty sure they would be a reasonable pool of welders around. We eventually bumped in to an English fabrication overseer based nearby who put us in touch with a fixer and between us we managed to round up a number of welders, who after some haggling agreed to a cash reward, obviously with the fixer's fee agreed.

The next problem was get together some kit such as welding rods, transformers and grinding tools. I sent a list of the more portable items to my superior at Aberdeen and one of my fabrication foremen and a Lloyds qualified inspector from Aberdeen who came to carry out final inspection brought several cases of equipment. By then my colleague from London had gone back to the UK so I had to drive up to the airport near Seville, a good distance away, to pick them up. Well into the journey I was pretty well lost. Pulling off the road I tried to read the pretty basic map I had when luck would have it two motorcycle policemen came by and questioned me as to where I was going and if I had any problems. The upshot was that they motored a short distance ahead of me and guided me right to the turn off at the airport!

We had quite a problem getting through the airport customs with all this unfamiliar equipment, the ultrasonic recorder with dials and switches seemed to be of particular interest to the customs staff. We had been warned to take care when motoring through a certain section near Seville as often when stopped at traffic lights bandits were wont to open the car door and snatch bags or purses or anything which looked of value. In fact such a thing happened, in darkness on the way back when stopped for a while at lights. One opened the door and noting the considerable heft of my two passengers thought better of it!

The riser units were laid out on the quay side with no repair facility or even electric points to connect up welding gear. This problem was solved by one our welders who found a manhole covering a duct with electric cables and junctions, and finding a live connection he just twisted the end of our cable on to it, dodging the sparks at the same time.

The risers were eighty feet long and thirty inches diameter with thick walls and large heavy connectors on each end, so were of considerable weight, all we had was a tiddly little forklift for handling. When moving a riser length we had to rig a long beam across the back of the forklift and we all hung on to add counterweight to the load on the forks. There was a busy fishmarket further along the quay, and numerous boats were berthed there and were coming and going.

I could see there was some tension when I took a walk along to the market with my camera one day. I think the reason being quite obvious when I took a look inside the market to see the fish laid out; it was clear that anything that was caught was landed and sold whatever the size. Later I spoke to the skipper of one of the boats and explained where I originally came from and reason for my interest, he then invited me aboard his vessel for a tour. The trawl rig on deck was completely different to Scottish boats and all seemed a bit rickety, but you could have eaten your dinner off the floorplates in the engine room. I think the word had got round as to the reason why I was there and met no animosity afterwards.

Each morning an elderly man used to come into the harbour area and walk all the way to the fish market, he was accompanied by a large black dog, it was obviously quite elderly as it walked very slowly and often it would be a long distance behind and frequently laid down for a rest dead to the world halfway as the weather was quite warm still at this time. On this particular occasion the roadway was being tarred, and would you believe it they tarred right over the sleeping dog! The flesh was gradually eaten away by vermin so by the time we left the ribs were still sticking up through the tarred surface of the road.

There was a small roadside café inside the entrance to the harbour that we used to go to for lunch, there was no menu, just a steak and bread, and red wine if requested. It was with some surprise we noted the drivers of 40ft artic lorries polishing off a bottle of red wine with their food and climb into the cab and drive away.

As were going to pay our workmen cash with no questions asked, I got head office to send over a courier with a load of

American Express cheques, which I could cash at a local bank. The first day I went to exchange these and told the teller the amount he immediately rushed me around to a side entrance and did the transaction in a back room, explaining that it was not advisable to be seen with such an amount of pesetas. At the completion of the job all the workmen came to our hotel and we took a side room to hand over the money.

Paco was the head barman and waiter there, and we had got to know him pretty well by this time. Any time we were having a few drinks at the bar, being favoured customers by that time, full measure was de rigueur. Knowing he liked whisky, when we said "have one yourself Paco" he would go to the back of the kitchen and open a small locked cupboard in the wall and pour himself a malt, obviously this was his stash and he was not going to be satisfied by the blended spirit available at the bar.

Another interesting interlude was when I had to make a trip to Port Elizabeth in South Africa. At the time our company had a licensing agreement with a company there who could manufacture various oilfield components to our designs and periodically someone from our works had to go there and check that all was as per agreement so that we could continue our connection.

The flight from UK to Johannesburg was non-stop as I recall but on return had to refuel, basically flying uphill so to speak! However, the journey from Johannesburg to Port Elizabeth seemed to take forever with some stops on the way. I always liked PE, as it was often known, having been there twice on my first trip in the merchant navy, as being right on the coast it was naturally much cooler than inland. My hotel, the Elizabethan, was on an elevated site with view of the harbour and sea.

The manager and supervisor of the company I was visiting were both from west of Scotland, no getting away from them, and were obviously glad to see someone from the old country which was the subject of many toasts during my visit. The fabrication shop was some way inland, in the bush as I would call it, and called for welly boots protection from snakes. The drive there from my hotel in PE took me past a building which was held to be the longest in the hemisphere.

They took me for a number of sightseeing tours, one I recall was a zoo, and my friend took a photo of me patting a cheetah, with my arm at full stretch I admit! During the visit we had to pay a call at Mossel Bay to inspect some of our equipment, a drive of about 200 miles south along the coast. The route was fairly tortuous with steep winding roads slowed by being behind numerous crawling lorries each loaded with three massive logs, so much so that the baboons along the side of the road would hop on and start to wrench the aerials.

Our stop-over was at a hotel at Plettenbug Bay, built on the style of a ship's bridge out on a projecting point in the sea. On hearing the barman talking I detected a more familiar tone, and learned his last posting had been the Gantock Hotel at Gourock in Scotland!

At the weekends the manager invited me to stay with them at their house, quite a way out of the town and fairly isolated, in fact it was only by their lights at night that the presence of other houses were revealed. They had three German Shepherd guard dogs, but regulations stipulated that any guns had to be locked in a safe.

After about seven years I had an opportunity to transfer to our base in Norway and spent a year there from August, 1984-85. Not a particularly rewarding period I confess, and having earlier had some short trips to our other base in Holland I leapt at the chance of a transfer there as plant manager. I think that the then European sales manager, whom I had got to know quite well in Aberdeen and who was in overall charge of the base in Holland, had a hand in requesting my transfer to his domain – for a number of reasons, later to become obvious, for which I am eternally grateful.

My move in August 1985 more or less coincided with my employers incorporating another company into our parent

Our house in Stavanger, Norway.

group, a move that naturally saw some rationalisation of conditions of employment etc. As frequently happens there is then a race to the bottom, with the least favourable conditions being adopted. In my case the expatriate terms which would apply to my new position in Holland were much less favourable than I was then currently enjoying, and naturally baulked at this unfavourable turn of events. My central argument was that had I, or anyone else for that matter, been working in Aberdeen and offered this contract we would have the opportunity to refuse, whereas I was already abroad and my only option as to accept the lesser terms or request to be returned to home base.

I think my above noted mentor made some representations to the powers above. Nevertheless I was a little surprised when the London-based vice president came across to Holland to listen to my concerns, and to give him credit he accepted that my situation was perhaps somewhat unique, and arranged for an amended and wholly satisfactory contract be implemented, but not forgetting to emphasise that I would be the last one to enjoy such bounty! My only comment was that the next one would have to fight their own battles! Whilst the employer will make some of the arrangements for any transfer these are by no means the whole story and a lot is left to the individual to do a lot of leg work to establish a new home and other domestic arrangements.

This factory was purposefully laid out and outfitted with machine tools ideally suited for welding of speciality connectors on drill casing tubulars and was served by an overhead crane which straddled the whole site with magnets attached to the hoists which could pick up three 20ins diameter by 40ft long casing pipes. We even had our own dedicated railway spur from a nearby harbour; thus loaded ships were chartered direct from Japan, discharged into rail wagons, and then travelled direct to our plant to be unloaded where we could handle thirteen at the time.

I did not anticipate any problems settling in at the workplace and the priority was to find somewhere to live, so my first visit was to estate agents to find out what was for rent to suit our requirements, and within the scale of company renting policy. Our works was in the south of Holland, about halfway between Rotterdam and Breda, so somewhere around Dordrecht seemed to be the best bet. After viewing a number of prospective houses it was time to narrow down to a final choice and to fetch Ruby over from Stavanger, for a final decision.

We finally settled on a house on the outskirts of Dordrecht, quite large and a few years old, with open farming fields out at the rear. The only possible snag on the horizon was that the owner had been transferred to work just close to the border in Germany, and at that time was unsure if he would be on an extended stay, but if not would definitely be back in six months. We decided to take the chance anyhow as we

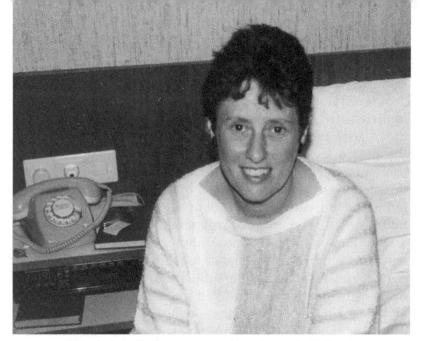

Ruby in hotel before we moved into house in Holland.

Back garden of our first house at Dordrecht in Holland

liked the locality as well. As it was only partially furnished my employers had to buy some items, here the often maligned Ikea came in handy.

One thing we failed to appreciate was the extreme cold of the winters in Holland. The living room was very large with a high ceiling, bare treated brick walls and tiled floor, and we soon found that the electric heaters were totally inadequate to heat sufficient for comfort, and had to be augmented by portable Calor gas heaters.

An illustration of the winter conditions is that an annual skating race was held on certain frozen canals which extended from the north of Holland to the south. We noted with some surprise one evening that the local fire brigade was flooding a number of fields nearby, the purpose was revealed next day when they were transformed into impromptu skating rinks.

In fact the winters in Holland felt much colder than in Stavanger, the cool air was coming from the European land mass, without the mitigating factor of a higher sea temperature to raise the temperature.

As I said, the house, in a row of about half a dozen, backed on to fields and a slout, or small canal, and it was common for a pair of ducks to waddle up and wash in a small pool in the back garden before having a snooze in the sun. Over a period of time a male pheasant was tame enough to come and feed at my feet, the female however stayed just out of reach.

This house had two sides almost completely glazed from floor to ceiling, fine in the summer but rather disconcerting in the winter with nothing but blackness outside, and open fields behind to boot. This was doubly so when I was frequently away at Aberdeen or other travels leaving Ruby alone, so curtains were eventually fitted. Curiously most householders in Holland are quite happy to have curtains fully open to expose the interior in the evening, even at street level; it is a matter of pride to show off their décor or fitments.

Another slight oddity was that we had a fully-fledged tree growing in the living room! There was an earthen trough which appeared to extend down to the subsoil, and watering was done by buckets and not watering cans. It was bending to seek the light from one of the glazed sides of the house, so much so that it was nearly impossible to open the large sliding doors.

The house was some way out of the town of Dordrecht, and before I was fully familiar with the local alternative traffic routes we were faced with a problem when coming back from the UK on one occasion. The return flight was late and by the time we reached Schipol Airport in Amsterdam it was after midnight, and a couple of hours later as we neared our destination we found that the roads were blocked off to allow them to be resurfaced. The workmen did their best to explain an alternative route, but it still took quite a while before we finally found our way via diversions to our house. Note re-surfacing was done overnight in Holland, no holding up traffic during working hours.

Flights from Rotterdam airports were enlivened by the extremely rigorous baggage search by a certain lady, everything spread out and examined in minute detail, her approach seemingly influenced by an antipathy to non-native Holland residents, my passport and Holland work permit being especially well scrutinised.

On one occasion one of our US senior staff was over on a visit to our plants in Aberdeen, Norway and Holland and somehow his luggage never reached this far, and due to the inevitable rush, arranging flights etc he had not been able to replenish his nether garments. His entreaty in his southern drawl to this formidable lady, intent on the usual vigorous examination, that "you really do not want to go there maam", was all to no avail unfortunately.

On our late return from the UK on another occasion on reaching my car in the long-stay car park at Schipol aerodrome in Amsterdam I immediately noted something odd about the door handle. The key slot had been burst open and I found that the radio had been stolen. This seemed to be common thing as I later realised when noting that the small square shoulder bag type satchel being carried by car owners after parking their car when visiting a supermarket etc was in fact a special bag for the radio, which was plugged into the dashboard.

An amusing, if annoying theft, occurred when one of our employee's car had been broken in and the radio stolen, the owner was a bit peeved to note that the thief obviously did not appreciate his taste in music as all the cassettes and discs had been spread out on the seat but not touched!

In the event the owner of our house in Dordrecht returned after six months, and we were on the move again, and the only house available was on a six-month lease. In the event this was a blessing as it turned out to be rather unsuitable in a number of ways. The owners were inveterate collectors of all kinds of knick-knacks and ornaments, so much so that a wall clock we had bought for the last house lay on a table for six months as there was literally not a space on any wall to hang it!

Our next house was in complete contrast, modern and unfurnished, but in a superb location overlooking the junction of the three major rivers in Holland, Oud, Maas and Waal, and from the balcony at the rear I could watch all the river traffic passing on the main internal routes to north east Holland and Germany and beyond. This was at Zwindrecht, just across the river from Dordrecht.

There was quite a sharp bend in the river passage at this point, and it was interesting to watch the pusher tugs, with a long train of laden barges lashed to the bow, crabbing sideways as they swung around the bend.

The house was unfurnished, apart from kitchen electrical items and white goods, so we had to start at the bottom and work up. On trips into Dordrecht for shopping it was more convenient to take the local road over an opening swing bridge or the small pedestrian ferry which criss-crossed the river from a terminal a short distance along the river bank from our house. Incidentally the house address was Westerschelde 11, so was easily remembered as Wester Skeld!

We were living more or less in central Holland, and convenient for travel in all directions, Sunday meant a trip up to the Central Station at Rotterdam to get the British Sunday newspapers and, in good weather, out to the river bank on the south side of the New Waterway to watch and photograph the shipping going up and down. Types ranged from the largest containers ships and tankers to all manner of coastal craft. Incredibly, in over three years I saw only three British registered ships – graphic evidence of the run-down of our merchant navy.

The period of nearly four years spent working in Holland was one of the most satisfying in my whole working life. Modern equipment and layout perfectly suitable for the product manufactured, and best of all, a loyal, hardworking and co-operative workforce, and I hope, and think, I showed the same consideration to them.

The fact that most could speak quite good English was a double-edged sword as if they heard me trying to speak in their language, as asking for something in a shop or directions, for example, they immediately switched to English! Soon after we moved to Holland we went in to the centre of Dordrecht to do some shopping, and noticing a butcher shop we went in and purchased some roast joint, which after cooking was most tasty. It was only some time later on passing the same shop when I was more familiar with the Dutch language I noticed the large sign "Pard" (pony) on the frontage, I never said anything to Ruby!

This reminds me of one occasion when we were awaiting an urgent delivery of some parts from Scotland, and I met the truck on arrival and queried the driver as to whether these were in the consignment. I naturally spoke to him in English whereupon he remarked: "It's amazing how you Dutch people can speak good English, and you have a Scots accent as well!" I never let on.

Such was the apparent smooth running of our plant that visits from my immediate boss, the general manager of manufacturing in Aberdeen, were few and far between; such that I kept a photo of him pinned up in my office to remember what he looked like! His comment was that "I only need to visit places where there are problems! I hoped I could take that as muted praise.

There was one memorable visit when I took him to a Greek restaurant, knowing he preferred quantity to quality, with the result that we ran up a considerable bill, unfortunately the establishment did not take American Express credit cards and neither of us had sufficient local currency to meet the final cost. Fortunately they accepted my business card with my assurance if they sent the bill to our works address it would be promptly paid.

Whilst in Holland accompanied by our quality manager I sometimes visited one of our subcontractors in the south of France. Lunch there in their canteen was a whole new experience, most of our hosts each polished off a full bottle of red wine, and a two hour lunch was regarded as a mere quick break.

We flew from Amsterdam to Paris and took a fast train from there to the works. My passage through the metal detector at the Paris airport was somewhat protracted, no matter what metals I emptied from my pockets the alarm kept being triggered, it was only when I realised that it was the steel safety toecaps in my shoes that was the reason – they were inside the toecaps of what looked like normal shoes – so you can imagine looks and muttering in French of the queue behind me. My colleague could speak perfect French and his translation of their comments to me later was to the effect "what is this crazy Englishman doing dressed in a suit with shirt and tie with steel shoes"!

Our local agent in Paris picked us up next morning from our overnight hotel to drive us to the airport, but when we reached where he was parked outside the hotel it appeared that his car was completely boxed in. To our surprise this did not faze him, the remedy being to not altogether gently bump the car ahead and behind alternatively to make room for his exit, on enquiry his explanation was that they did not apply the handbrake when parking. On learning that, my colleague and I had some amusement later noting the state of the front and rear bumpers on many cars.

Travel always seemed to throw up some surprises as illustrated when flying from Amsterdam to Glasgow. The flight was delayed by several hours and in the end cancelled and I was re booked via London. During the long wait in the airport I got chatting to another lad from Glasgow so we kept company on arrival at London. By this time, after the long delay and no meals in Holland and long wait for our next flight to Glasgow, we were a bit peckish and the bar had not opened so we were a little frazzled. However, whilst waiting we observed passengers being decanted from a delayed outward bound holiday charter flight and being ushered by holiday reps en-masse into a dining room and could overhear them advising that this meal was to mitigate the inconvenience of the delay.

I looked at my companion and said are you thinking what I am thinking? We joined the queue and found seats at a table and waited to be served. Our initiative was not rewarded however, the steak was barely edible, the wine only downed with a grimace. Expressing his sympathy with our delayed holiday, and to our horror, the waiter topped up our glasses again!

Next embarrassment came when us two single men, in rather formal dress, and each with an overcoat and a briefcase, contrasting with the more casual holiday attire of the others going on holiday somewhere warm was obviously attracting some attention. The couple at the next table, quite conversationally, told us where they were staying and asked which hotel we were booked in at. We bluffed this one out by saying it was a last-minute decision and would only find out on arrival.

Whilst living in Holland my wife and I flew to Denia in Spain for a holiday. We were on a charter holiday flight full of Dutch people travelling as a group and when in the queue on arrival in Spain we presented our British passports some confusion ensued, we were assumed to have strayed into the wrong section and they took some convincing that we actually lived in Holland.

An added bonus was that Holland as a whole perfectly suited my interests with a distinct maritime environment, such as museums, harbours, and all kinds of craft from the smallest sailing to largest afloat easily observed within close reach. Additionally I had no worries about Ruby being on her own when I was at work as she always felt perfectly safe whenever shopping or travelling by ferry or bridge across the river to Dordrecht.

Travelling to work took about three-quarters of an hour via a motorway. There was, however, only one downside to the location of our house which was highlighted when joining the motorway each morning. The position of the on-ramp meant that I had to cross several lanes of fast moving traffic within a very short distance to join the correct lane to take me to place of work at Moerdijk, the adrenaline was certainly pumping on dark mornings timing my lateral manoeuvres and dodging the speeding traffic. I admit to hearing a few blasts of car horns from irate drivers

The time in Holland passed all too quickly and after nearly four years it was time to move back to the UK. I had mixed feelings as I had nothing but good memories of Holland and the people. The near four years I spent there was one of the happiest and most rewarding of my working life.

Truth to tell the time spent after the move back to my original workplace did not turn out to be the happiest. I think that being my own boss so to speak in Holland, where you could use your own initiative with short chains of command provided it conformed broadly to the company's policies, contrasted with the more hierarchical and structured approach which did not sit well after so long away from home base.

It was often held in the company that some members of their personnel who had spent some years in a foreign location often "went native", if that description fits then I suppose I have to plead guilty. After about a year back at home base I decided that this was not for me and took my leave with severance.

I worked in a variety of jobs for the next year until, most fortuitously and in the summer of 1989, I was offered a position as operations manager by my old employers, the John Swire group. By this time they had a large base in Aberdeen for supply, rental and repair of offshore containers, helifuel and chemical tanks. The local chief executive was an old colleague from our days working for Swire in Greenock in the 1970s.

This turned out to be a perfect move to end my working career, a well-run and well-respected company with co-operative employees and having the backing of a large well established multi-national company with a strong ethos of excellence, safety culture and general all-round competence. The backing of the parent group certainly allowed us to procure the best tools and other equipment and have our rental containers and tanks etc updated and kept in first class condition.

One example of the considerable outlay was the purchase of a number of large fork lift trucks from Kalmar in Sweden, a noted specialist in the field of mechanical handling. With their UK-based sales representative I was sent over to Sweden to check the new units before despatch, and whilst there one of their staff invited to us to witness their automatic robot controlled paint shop. The components were each placed on hooks which were attached to moving rails to pass through the paint booth, the operator would then enter the relevant unit part number on a computer which would then send a signal to the robot which would in turn manipulate the nozzle to ensure all surfaces were coated. On completion of the cycle he would proudly show us the result. I noted a thin strip of bare metal on each of the components whereupon he replied that this was where the hook was attached and they had not quite cracked that problem just yet!

At this point it may be relevant to record some impressions of my experiences of various nationalities as workmates and colleagues, all gained from periods spent in the course of my working career in a number of countries.

It would be unfair to categorise a whole nation from contact with any one individual or small sample. For example, the interaction with your shipmates in such a closed environment as onboard a ship can have a disproportionate influence compared to a job where you can leave and go home at the end of the working day. Much as it pains me I have to admit, if taking a group of workmates where we all had our faults, if there was one in a group who was particularly uncooperative or even downright obnoxious it was one of my own countrymen!

I found the Dutch in particular excellent colleagues as epitomised by the co-operation I enjoyed during the near four years I spent in Holland as plant manger of our works. Should a job have to be done in a certain critical timeframe I was confident that it would be completed, and if not then it would not be for the want of application or effort. As I was the lone Brit there it could have been so very difficult if we had not struck up an effective accord and good working relationships at all levels in the facility.

There were certain customs that may appear strange to us here. For example it was quite normal to celebrate birthdays outwith the usual 21st with the marking of decades, and presents of flowers to the recipient, male or female. This had an amusing sequel when working back in Aberdeen after returning from Holland. I passed through our reception area after lunch one day when the receptionist surreptitiously beckoned me into her office and, indicating a big bunch of flowers sent from Holland with a birthday card addressed to me attached, commented that she did not want to put it in my office in full view. You can well image the thoughts going through her mind until I explained that this was a common practice in Holland.

I spent a considerable time associating with Americans in the course of my work afloat and on land, and the overall impression at times was a certain naivety in some aspects in comparison with ourselves. Perhaps this was due to the size of the country where in some cases the individual had never been outside the Texas or the Californian boundary. The novelty of passports and their surprise at the amount of green on the ground in the UK seemed strange to us.

Whilst much of the pioneering work on oil production in all its phases had been carried out in the USA we found that as time passed in our Aberdeen manufacturing plant – a wholly owned American facility – we instigated a number of manufacturing processes well in advance of our sister facilities in California and Texas, especially in the deeper waters of the North Sea and more northerly aspects of drilling and production processes.

It was noticeable that our manufacturing foremen in Aberdeen had a greater scope to use their own initiative at times in the interest of efficiency rather than slavishly follow written procedures. This could possibly be a result of them having had an applicable apprenticeship in contrast to many of their USA counterparts but in respect of co-operation and general attitude I found them excellent to work with.

My time in the merchant navy was with a shipping company that employed UK officers and Indian or Pakistani deck, catering and engineering crews. My experience was that provided you treated them with same respect as you would your countrymen in similar positions there was no problem, albeit recognising that at times the differing language may inadvertently cause some misunderstanding rather than any reluctance to carry out an order. In fact the company was particularly acutely aware of the negative atmosphere which would result from any such discrimination and took pains to ensure correct and fair treatment of these nationals.

BACK TO BOATS AGAIN

Living at Greenock on the south bank of the lower reaches of the Clyde I was familiar with the many yachts and pleasure craft prevalent there. The nearby sheltered lochs and picturesque scenery around the Argyll coast provided a perfect backdrop for yachting. My first foray was when I built one of the very popular Mirror dinghies, sail number 15,263, designed by the well-known dinghy sailor and designer Jack Holt. This was built from a kit on the stitch and glue principle which included just about everything to get afloat, then costing £61.50 as I recall.

Whilst we were living in a second floor flat I was fortunate that there was a large unused washroom in the basement opening out onto the back yard which was ideal to build the craft. The problem arose however when completed was how to get the finished craft up the narrow angled staircase to street level. However by dint of some delicate manoeuvring with help I was able to get up the stairs and on to the roof rack of my trusty Morris Minor 1000 car.

This craft served the family for a couple of years of happy sailing but, recognising its limitations, I hankered for something bigger. I then noted an advert in *The Glasgow Herald* describing a Shetland built clinker double-ended sailing cabin cruiser for sale, stored ashore at Sandbank at Dumbarton. Further enquiry revealed that she had been built in 1958 by the well-known Shetland boatbuilder Jess Goudie at Port Arthur in Scalloway, then as the *Henrietta* for a doctor in Aberdeen. At this time however she was named *Corrie*. Recognising her pedigree I had no qualms as to her quality although some neglect meant that renovation was required.

My first boat. I built this Mirror dinghy sail no. 15,263.

Shetland model *Auk* sailing on the Clyde. Built by Jess Goudie in 1958.

Over the next couple of years I carried out some refurbishment and brought her back to something like her original, including repainting the all-black hull to a more preferable white and renamed her *Auk*. Naturally this boat offered more scope for exploring the many lochs and anchorages around the lower Clyde estuary. However wooden boats inevitably demand more maintenance and upkeep and to due to time constraints I somewhat reluctantly put her up for sale.

Incidentally, later I found out that she was owned by a Pottinger lady from Edinburgh who had close family connections in Branchiclate and Southerhouse in Burra. Many years later I tracked this boat as being laid up at Balvicar on the island of Seil, having had the deck removed and other modifications, but is now currently she is being rebuilt as original at Lochgilphead.

Once bitten by the bug it was not long before I started looking around for a more suitable craft and was lucky to be able to purchase an 18ft GRP transom sterned boat, the hull having been made by the well-known Tyler builders. She had been fitted with an 8bhp Stuart Turner inboard engine, narrow side decks and short foredeck with small shelter open at after end and was complete with launching and transportable trailer. As the owner lived at Kilcreggan across the Clyde a friend towed the boat back to Greenock via the road around the Gareloch, through Helensburgh, Dumbarton and across the Erskine Bridge.

Fortunately I had access to a vacant store at my workplace and over the next winter fitted a proper enclosed deckhouse complete with seat berths, table and the other necessary fittings to be habitable for cruising. The conversion was completed by making mast and spars to suit a small set of sails from the well-known sailmakers Jeckells which had been part of a cancelled order and luckily were just the size for the boat. It was accepted that this rig would not give great performance under sail, especially to windward, with a hull of this type but was more than adequate with a wind anywhere from amidships to aft.

The *Aurora*, as she was renamed, gave many happy days afloat with family, and also when once each summer I spent a week with two former apprentice pals cruising as far as Tarbert, Loch Fyne, with overnight stops at a number of ideal anchorages amid beautiful scenery. An aside which gives some indication of how Swire operated was when working on this boat in this store after work one early evening. The late

Sir Adrian Swire, son of John Swire, had been up at Greenock visiting our works and whilst on a plant tour with our manager happened to be passing the store where I was working and noting the light shining out the door asked what was in there. I was duly introduced and he was then appraised as to what I was doing before going on their way.

It must have been at least 20 years later when I was back working for Swire in Aberdeen that Sir Adrian was being taken round by our chief executive and I was again introduced. He looked at me a little quizzically and said: "Are you not the fellow I saw working on your boat at Greenock last time we met?"

Aurora, I fitted her out from a bare hull.

RETIRAL

The Swire policy was for retiral at sixty but as no replacement for me had been found I was asked to carry on for another year. This I did but only working three days each week, which was an ideal way to gradually ease into retirement. In some ways however this was a double-edged sword as I found myself doing in three days what I would do in five! Tale had it was I was either working very hard in the three days or not very hard previously when working five days!

During my last year in 1994 we moved to a larger house in an excellent setting in Bridge of Don, with added bonus of having a large gated area adjoining which was ideal for keeping our caravan. We had bought a motor home previously and toured extensively in Scotland. I bought this vehicle from an elderly gentleman who obviously looked on it as his pride and joy, the side window curtains were still in the original wrappers, all external chromium fittings had been coated with varnish preservative, and he had a log book of every monetary transaction. During a test run he sat beside me and literally duplicated every gear change and change of course.

When it came to payment in response to my offer of a cheque he averred that "I never have much to do with a bank"! Oddly enough many years later I discovered this same vehicle when caravanning in the North East of Scotland, the then owner had replaced the original petrol engine with a diesel, the bodywork and fittings obviously meriting the upgrade.

Whilst comfortable to drive it was a bit of a chore packing every moveable thing away each time we moved however briefly, so I decided to exchange it for a new caravan which was more comfortable and roomy but a chore to tow on some routes.

Our last house in Bridge of Don, Aberdeen.

For most of the summer months we kept the caravan on a site a Findochty, on the Moray coast, a site convenient for further travels and saving towing back home to and fro each weekend. The circumstances relating to the decision to use this site came about in a curious manner. On booking in on first visit the warden, a retired fisherman, commented that he had met me before somewhere, it turned out that I had done a painting for him of a trawler he was then skippering, the *River Dee*, a good number of years previously. One thing led to another and he asked me to do a painting of the minesweeper HMS *Bronington* as whilst still in the Royal Navy Reserve he had served on the ship at same time as Prince Charles. I was only too happy to oblige and in return we agreed favourable terms for extended site rental for the caravan each summer.

We kept this caravan for a number of years when it became a question of buying a larger one or calling it a day as far as our caravanning was concerned, in the end we decided to stop. Our house was in a prime location with a walled boundary giving a secluded gardens and mature bushes and trees all round which we added to with flowers, conservatory and patio with the added bonus that we were soon friendly with all the neighbours, in all the perfect spot to enjoy one's retiral.

Our son Jim had graduated from Aberdeen University with a BSc Honours degree in Chemistry in July 1982, and the following year with a Masters degree at Bristol University, his wife to be, Kate, having graduated there with a BSc Honours in Chemistry in 1982. Jim and Kate were married in 1995 and our granddaughter Phoebe India was born two years later. Recently, whilst at Birmingham University studying medicine, Phoebe took a year out from the university to attend and graduate from King's College, London, with a First Class Honours Degree in Women's Health and Basic Medical Sciences, and is now in final year back at Birmingham to complete her studies.

**Son Jim's graduation at Aberdeen University, July 1982,
second from left back row.**

Granddaughter Phoebe's graduation
photo at Kings College in July 2019.

Phoebe at Largs in August 2020.

Happy first meeting with Kate our daughter-in-law to be.

Sadly our wedded bliss was be ended when Ruby gradually succumbed to that most horrible of ailments, Alzheimer dementia and its associated problems. I cared for her at home for many months until it became too much and she then spent a short period in hospital whilst waiting until I made arrangements for her to enter a care home quite close to our house. This period was especially stressful as the policy was for me to inspect at least three establishments and hopefully find one that met requirements as regards access and general suitability.

It is perhaps easy to criticise, and I fully appreciate the difficulties inherent in providing a suitable level of care for patients in various degrees of impairment, but I felt some could not give me the peace of mind that Ruby would be looked after to a standard that I would be comfortable with. In the end I was fortunate to find a nearby establishment in February 2015 which had been purpose built as a care home and she stayed there until her passing on 7th May of that year. It may seem callous to say, but in the end I think it was a blessing for both of us seeing that her quality of life was quickly deteriorating. My only consolation was that her very last words when conscious was when she said to one of the nurses: "I have a good husband!"

The experience of observing the daily routine in this care home certainly opened my eyes just to the level of attention and dedication in the most trying circumstances as displayed by the staff at all levels. The rest of May that year was a bit of a blur with trying to come to terms with the cessation of married life a few weeks short of 57 years.

Later in May, as usual every year, I went to the annual fishery exhibition held in Bridge of Don in Aberdeen to meet old contacts and have a general look around, and it was there when chatting to my nephew Jerry, skipper on the fishing trawler *Venture*, that he said "why do you not move back to Shetland, there is nothing left for you here"

I had not really thought about it in such terms with all that happened recently but it was not long before Janice, his wife, phoned to give details of some houses likely to be of interest.

To cut a long story short I bought a modern three bedroom bungalow with double garage house, not quite off plan, but off photos so to speak! Moving back to Shetland on the 16th October, 2015, I knew the locality and it was quite close to my near relatives. The unobstructed view of the open sea out to the west and a big garage was a real plus as was moving from a much larger house and a lot could be stored there until I could decide what was for keeping and what was not. I admit to being an inveterate hoarder, especially bits of wood (never know when it may come handy sometime!) and books. When we moved back to Aberdeen from Holland I had packed no less than 14 boxes of books!

This was quite a big step, and I talked it over with my son, who with his family lived in Yorkshire. Obviously this would greatly extend the distance between us, where he lived was especially nice but too far from the sea for me and in the end he accepted that and we decided it was for the best as I would be among my roots and people I knew.

After moving back to Shetland I had never really thought about owning a boat until talking to Brian Anderson one day about the boats I had owned previously when living on the Clyde. He asked if I had never thought of getting a boat again. I have to admit a certain longing when seeing craft afloat on a fine summer day, but never really considered it. I happened to mention to him I had noted a certain boat lying on the shore at Port Arthur in Scalloway, a type I had long admired for looks and construction.

It was perhaps inevitable that this would set the ball rolling as about two weeks later he phoned me to tell that this boat was for sale! To cut a long story short I was soon the owner of a Dell Quay Fisher Boat, some 20 ft overall with inboard diesel engine. Whilst the internal woodwork was pretty well gone I made some temporary repairs to allow me to use her for that summer.

Luckily my garage was large enough to keep her inside all next winter when I stripped all internals out to the bare shell and more or less rebuilt the boat and named her *Ruby*, the result being that I was able to berth in a nearby marina and to enjoy some wonderful outings to the various islands close at hand.

My last boat, a Dell Quay Fisher, I had to rebuild the whole inside.

FINALE

We had visited Shetland intermittently previously and noted the changes to Burra and Hamnavoe in particular. All a striking contrast to when I left for the first time in 1951, with many modern houses and renovations carried out on the original traditional but and bens. No matter how the advent of the bridges to the Shetland mainland was viewed at the time of construction, and it was not universally welcomed, I would contend that without it the younger people of working age would gradually have drifted off to the mainland. With the now common usage of cars it is now possible to live here and work in many areas of Shetland.

Whilst not a backwater by any means, after a lifetime in a variety of places and countries I find the pace of life has a certain calmness with people taking the time to speak and, whilst hoping not to be offering a hostage to fortune, not having to lock up everything.

I found it especially noticeable the number of thriving locally based community organisations and activities, having lived most of my adult life in large cities where, while there may have been similar activities it was not as evident in comparison. It is striking to note the large sums of money raised locally for the MRI scanner for example.

It is perhaps illustrative that when my daughter-in-law and granddaughter first visited a few years ago they noted that when driving and meeting people on foot they would hold up their hand or wave in recognition. She wondered if I knew all these people. I had to explain that no, I did not, but that this was just the Shetland way.

Having literally missed two generations I really only really readily recognise those of a certain age, and offer due apologies to those not recognised. Sadly the number of my contemporaries is diminishing every year.

Above: Hamnavoe beach front in the mid 1960s. Our house was in the middle in line with the pole at the beach. Below: Hamnavoe, 2018.

Hamnavoe at dusk before the marina was built.

BV - #0006 - 290721 - C18 - 210/148/7 - PB - 9781910997338 - Gloss Lamination